Contemporary Artificial Art and the Law

Art and Law

Volumes published in this Brill Research Perspectives title are listed at *brill.com/rpal*

Contemporary Artificial Art and the Law

Searching for an Author

By

Gianmaria Ajani

BRILL

LEIDEN | BOSTON

This paperback book edition is simultaneously published as issue 3.4 (2019) of *Art and Law*, DOI:10.1163/24684309-12340009

Library of Congress Control Number: 2020914633

Typeface for the Latin, Greek, and Cyrillic scripts: "Brill". See and download: brill.com/brill-typeface.

ISBN 978-90-04-44266-5 (paperback)
ISBN 978-90-04-44268-9 (e-book)

This book is printed on acid-free paper and produced in a sustainable manner.

Contents

Contemporary Artificial Art and the Law

Searching for an Author

Gianmaria Ajani
University of Torino, Italy
gianmaria.ajani@unito.it

Abstract

The advent of Artificial Intelligence as an "autonomous author" in the various modes of Arts urges the law to rethink the traditional concepts of authorship, originality, and creativity. AI-generated artworks are in search of an author, so to speak, because current copyright laws only offer the solution of the public domain or fragile regulatory mechanisms. Several adjustments have globally led copyright laws to cover new forms of authorship as well as new sorts of works. Yet, the romantic idea of a lone individual as the master of creativeness still influences theoretical elaborations and normative choices. Throughout the 20th century, visual artists have been posing persistent challenges to the law: conceptual art and dematerialization have favored legal mechanisms alternative to copyright law. The case of AIart is, however, different: for the first time, the art world is discovering the perspective of an art without human authors. Rather than preserving the status quo in the legal world, policy makers should consider a reformative conception of AI in copyright law and take inspiration from innovative theories in the field of robot law, where new frames for a legal personhood of artificial agents are proposed. This would also have a spill-over effect on copyright regulations.

Keywords

contemporary art – artificial intelligence – copyright law – authorship – creativity

1 Introduction

From Mary Shelley's Frankenstein's Monster to the classical myth of Pygmalion, through the story of Prague's Golem to the robot of Karel Čapek, who coined the word, people have fantasised about the

 | DOI:10.1163/9789004442689_002

> possibility of building intelligent machines, more often than not androids with human features.[1]

This quote from a recent EU Parliament resolution recaps a set of old stories; today, those *fantasies* have been developed into complex technologies, called Artificial Intelligence (AI).[2]

---

1 *Civil Law Rules on Robotics – European Parliament resolution of 16 February 2017, with recommendations to the Commission on Civil Law Rules on Robotics* (2015/2103 (INL)).

2 Artificial Intelligence (AI) is defined by the International Organization for Standardization (ISO) as "The capacity of data processing systems to perform functions normally associated with human intelligence, such as reasoning, learning, and self-improvement" (ISO/IEC JTC 1/SC 42 – Artificial intelligence). Within this frame, it is essential to distinguish AI systems based on the processes of predictive data analytics, big data and data mining from AI systems processing data independently of the user.

It is this last application of AI-based technologies that brings the greatest challenge to some established notions in the vocabulary of Law and Arts, such as *authorship*, *creativity*, *originality*.

The next step in the advancement of AI is expected to be *Artificial general intelligence* (AGI): the *speculative* intelligence of a machine that has the capacity to understand or learn any intellectual task that a *human being* can. AGI is also referred to as *strong AI*, *full AI*, *or general intelligent action*. *Strong AI* will be able to learn by itself, and therefore autonomously upgrade, without any instructions from human actors. Therefore, the maker of the AGI will not be in charge of programming a machine's options or outcomes. For a scholarly definition of Artificial Intelligence, see Stuart P. Russell and Peter Norvig (*Artificial Intelligence. A Modern Approach*, 4rd ed., Pearson 2020, pp. 1–2). According to the authors, the term "Artificial Intelligence" can be defined following four different approaches: thinking humanly (which measures closeness to human thought processes); thinking rationally (measuring the thought process against an ideal performance embodied in rationality); acting humanly (measuring fidelity to human behavior); acting rationally (where it is considered that a system is rational if it does the "right thing").

As a sample normative definition of AI see *U.S. National Defense Authorization Act for Fiscal Year 2019* Sect. 238(g): "In this section, the term 'artificial intelligence' includes the following:

(1) Any artificial system that performs tasks under varying and unpredictable circumstances without significant human oversight, or that can learn from experience and improve performance when exposed to data sets.

(2) An artificial system developed in computer software, physical hardware, or other context that solves tasks requiring human-like perception, cognition, planning, learning, communication, or physical action.

(3) An artificial system designed to think or act like a human, including cognitive architectures and neural networks.

(4) A set of techniques, including machine learning, that is designed to approximate a cognitive task.

(5) An artificial system designed to act rationally, including an intelligent software agent or embodied robot that achieves goals using perception, planning, reasoning, learning, communicating, decision making, and acting".

Since the 1970s computers have been employed to produce all sorts of imaginative works, such as paintings, drawings, poems, musical compositions, etc. Most of those computer-made *oeuvres* derived from the programmer's inputs, and the machine was meant to be a simple instrument, like a brush or a camera.[3] This perception persists today, but at the same time we are now facing a dramatic technological change, that gives us cause to re-evaluate the role played by processors in the creative course. When computers were appropriately considered as nothing more than a tool,[4] legal provisions were applied accordingly. Most of today's AI-driven mechanisms develop algorithms through the use of machine learning: the separation of machines from humans therefore brings a new challenge to an established set of provisions on law and the arts.

The advent of supercomputing and microprocessors in the early 1970s produced a response both in the legal and in the philosophical literature. However, this response was not identical. While normative choices and scholarly opinions identified computers as nothing more than an instrument serving the mind and the hand of an author, the theoretical debate in philosophy and epistemology circles continued to express the mood initiated by Alan Turing on the possibility of a qualitative leap in artificial intelligence. That separation has not been mended. Today the legal world insists on AI being an instrument, an object useful to create other items, rather than a subject. On the other hand, many disciplines have converged investigating the frontiers of AI and the interactions between humans and machines.

As Italo Calvino insightfully wrote:

> Will we have a machine capable of replacing the poet and the author? [...]. The interesting thing is not so much the question whether this problem is soluble in practice [...] as the theoretical possibility of it, which would give rise to a set of unusual conjectures [...]. Nothing prevents us from foreseeing a literature machine that a certain point feels unsatisfied

---

3 On the early experiments made in the 1970s by artist and art professor Harold Cohen, see Richard Moss, *Creative AI: The Robots that Would Be Painters*. http://newatlas.com/creative-ai-algorithmic-art-painting-fool-aaron/36106/ (February 28, 2020, last visit).

4 "In retrospect we know that the AI project couldn't possibly have succeeded at that stage (i.e. the early 1970s). The hardware was simply not powerful enough.[...] The computers in the seventies had a computing power comparable to that of insects. They also achieved approximately insect-level intelligence", Nick Bostrom, "How Long Before Superintelligence", 2 *Int. J. Future Stud.* 1998, p. 7.

> with its own traditionalism and starts to propose new ways of writing, turning its own codes completely upside down.[5]

Currently, literature in both liberal arts and Information Technologies (IT) hosts contributions suggesting important changes to be made in copyright laws,[6] so as to keep up with new technologies. Artworks generated by AI systems have received much attention from the public and the media: we are becoming familiar with a new connotation of the expression *Generative Art*, namely *AI-Generated Art*. Some generative artists, keen on questioning conventional notions about authorship, opted for leaving the making of artworks to a machine.

Traditionally, *Generative art* referred to:

> any art practice where the artist uses a system, such as a set of natural language rules, a computer program, a machine, or other procedural invention, which is set into motion with some degree of autonomy contributing to or resulting in a completed work of art.[7]

When confronted with new challenges brought by AI-generated works, the law finds itself in an awkward predicament – a similar situation already occurred with respect to conceptual art.[8] Most commentators refer to the letter of the law, where a "human factor" seems to be an inescapable requirement of authorship. Others minimize the matter, noting the rarity of judicial cases where AI-generated art is at stake.

In my view, a debate on the impact of AI on copyright laws is significant and should not be postponed based on the excuse of the immaturity, if not

5 Italo Calvino, *The Literature Machine. Essays* (1980), trans. by Patrick Craig, New York: Random House, 1997, p. 8.

6 When using "copyright laws" as a general expression I am not referring to a particular national or international legal order, but rather to normative choices shared by most legal systems in the world.

7 Philip Galanter, "XEPA: Intelligent Sculptures as Experimental Platforms for Computational Aesthetic Evaluation", www.philipgalanter.com (2013). Galanter notes that "generative art preceded computer art, and in fact is as old as art itself. Equally important is the virtual certainty that new forms of generative art will come after the computer as well. Nanotechnology, genetic engineering, robotics, and other technologies will no doubt offer generative artists some wonderful opportunities".

8 On the many challenges brought to copyright law by conceptual artists see, extensively, Alessandra Donati, *Law and Art: Diritto Civile e Arte Contemporanea*, Milan: Giuffré, 2012, pp. 11–53.

irrelevance, of the topic. Generative AI systems and the artworks that they produce raise policy concerns. These concerns affect ownership entitlements and the legal protection of artists, researchers, engineers who are experimenting in the field. Also, AI-generated creations question the dynamics among art producers, artworks and the public. The aim of this essay is to attest that, far from being unripe, the matter is incumbent and relevant for the global (and national) legal regulations of art production.

Authors' rights have been governed, since the late 19th century, by a mix of international covenants and national laws. As a matter of fact, legal scholars tend to agree that an adjustment in the letters of the law, if not a wider reform of its scope, is needed whenever there is an increase in litigation. Judicial adjudication of conflicts is a reliable meter to detect a demand for new regulation, or for amendments to the one in place.

Alternatively, deficiencies or gaps in the regulation can be made up for by resorting to alternative measures, such as settlements, voluntary mediation or arbitration, or by drafting contracts and similar sets of formal documents, to mark the existence of an artistic action. This last remedy has been practiced, for instance, by conceptual artists: the absence of a clearly identifiable output as a result of the artistic process proved to be quite problematic for the law, accustomed to treat artworks as items, artefacts – in a word, *objects*. When observing how AI-generated art impacts the system of regulations which we can refer to as *classic copyright law*, we find drawings and paintings, or songs, novels and poems. The missing element is not on the side of the output: rather, it is on the side of the *author*.

There is no pile of pending cases on the issue of recognizing copyright to machines. Perhaps there isn't one *yet*, because classic copyright law has an answer to the question of authorless-artworks: *public domain*. This is, however, a kind of default solution, not designed to govern the specific issue of AI-generated art. A time-limited economic privilege assisted by permanent moral rights is, though declined in different modes, a pattern common to every legal order on the globe. There is no space, within this pattern, for non-human authors. However, while creations made by humans with the aid of a machine, until recently, could be easily qualified as the result of human creativity, new technologies allow today for *independently AI-generated outputs*.

An increasing production of AI-generated artefacts is flanked by a growing literature centered on the need to provide legal protection to those *oeuvres*. And here we have the conundrum: copyright law is about motivating authors to create, while providing protection to their work. Machines do not need to be motivated; at the same time, their independence from human intervention can lead to unexpected aesthetic results.

The awkwardness of the law does not deter the production and sale of AI-independently generated works, nor does it inhibit the institutions of the art world, like galleries and auction houses, from introducing these works as AI-authored. In fact, slowness or absence of regulation usually does not inhibit the functioning of markets. If artificial art is in search of an author and the law is not able to satisfy this request, we can expect, as mentioned, increased litigation or the recourse to alternative measures on a case by case basis.

This essay contends that it is time to set forth on refocusing copyright laws related to new technologies. A simple readjustment, as already done in the past, would not be satisfactory; further harmonization is needed, which cannot be provided by *ad hoc* changes. Moreover, a set of challenging and original perspectives on the legal status of independent artificial agents is being developed within the field of the Law and Regulation of Robots.[9] Those perspectives should not be left out of a desirable discussion on AI-made art and new copyright law.

The proposed topic is, by its nature, interdisciplinary; accordingly, the intended audience of this essay consists not only of experts in the law of copyrights, but also of artists and curators active in the field of art and technology; authorship and originality are two classic themes in the philosophy of art and therefore those working in this field are also expected to be part of the readership.

The content of the Parts to follow mirrors this necessary interdisciplinarity: Part 2 offers a view on some manifestations of AI-made *visual* art and considers how these are related to copyright laws. Part 3 deals with the qualification of authorship between the law and the practice of visual arts. Part 4 brings the historical discourse on authorship in contact with the emergence of the artificial in art-making. Part 5 examines the traditional, and circular, discourse about authorship, originality and creativity which structures copyright laws and addresses the need to recognize creativity in some kinds of AI-driven machines. In conclusion, Part 6 draws the line between the world of the law and the practice of the art world on the qualification of AI-independently made artefacts, suggesting that changes to copyright regulations should take into consideration both the art practice and the perspectives brought by the literature on the legal status of AI-driven robots.

9 See Ugo Pagallo, "As Law Goes By: Topology, Ontology, Evolution", in Pompeu Casanovas, Ugo Pagallo, Giovanni Sartor, Gianmaria Ajani, *AI Approaches to the Complexity of Legal Systems*, Dordrecht: Springer, 2010, pp. 12–26.

2 Artificial Art in Search of an Author[10]

As Annemarie Brady has vividly noted:

> Today, artists, copyright professionals, producers, curators are facing a new challenge. Instead of waiting for a possible, and, quite seemingly, delayed and fragmented, intervention by an international regulator, they could take the opportunity and open the discussion for a more general reframing of a Global Copyright Law for the 21st century. Perhaps, the (so far) relatively slow development of AI offers a make-up from the reactive, crisis-driven model of policymaking that has so far governed copyright law in the digital era.[11]

Imagination, creativity, and therefore artmaking: these abilities are peculiar to human intelligence and vibrant marks of humankind.[12] Among the three, imagination precedes creativity in the development of human consciousness, while creativity may, but not necessarily does, reflect itself in a product. And this product could be a tool, a tale, an artwork.

At first the law paid little attention to creativity as such, and for ages the production and trade of its results have been regulated by using the two main tools of private law: property and contracts. Later on, concurrently with the first industrial revolution in Europe, creativity began to be perceived as an important mover for human progress; this has been the main reason adopted by politicians to establish copyright regimes. Nowadays, the so-called 4th revolution[13]

10 2021 will be the centennial of the first performance of *Six Characters in Search of an Author*. The title of the present essay is inspired by Luigi Pirandello's naming of his landmark play. (As is known, its first performance in Rome was met with harsh incomprehension: the audience disrupted the show shouting "Madhouse!". Already in 1922, however, the play was welcomed to Broadway, and within a few years it was received with admiration in Europe and the United States).

11 Annemarie Bridy, "Coding Creativity: Copyright and the Artificially Intelligent Author", 5 *Stan. Tech. L. Rev.*, 2012, p. 5.

12 Emanuel Jauk, Mathias Benedek, Beate Dunst, Aljoscha C. Neubauer, "The Relationship between Intelligence and Creativity: New Support for the Threshold Hypothesis by Means of Empirical Breakpoint Detection", in 41 *Intelligence*, July 4 2013, pp. 212–221.

A neat scholarly definition of creativity was provided by Jessica Fjeld and Mason Kortz, "A Legal Anatomy of AI-generated Art: Part I", *Harvard J. L. & Tech.*, November 2017, 1. https://jolt.law.harvard.edu/digest/a-legal-anatomy-of-ai-generated-art-part-i.

13 See Luciano Floridi *The Fourth Revolution. How the Infosphere is Reshaping Human Reality*, Oxford: OUP, 2014.

is boosted by the development of machine learning[14] and deep learning software, subsets of the AI process, capable of driving autonomous systems to learn and execute outputs (like poetry, novels, drawings) without being explicitly instructed by human beings:

> this development re-imagines the whole concept of art and artists and as such it has resulted in the need to re-create the legal regime that governs art, especially artworks produced by AI systems.[15]

While arguing that the traditional laws of copyright are inadequate to cope with the new technology involved in creating artworks, Shlomit Yanisky-Ravid contends that *oeuvres* autonomously generated by machines challenge a basic tenet of copyright law, namely that only humans can create works:

> Copyright laws are simply ill-equipped to accommodate this tech-revolution and are therefore unlikely to survive in their current form. In order to address the change in the way art is being created, we must either rethink these laws, give them new meaning, or be ready to replace them.[16]

This has gone side by side with the constant evolution of data mining technologies:

> In contrast to early AI, deep learning technologies afford computers capacities to collate and organize information, to make intelligent

---

14 A formal definition of Machine Learning is given by Tom Mitchell: "A computer programme is said to learn from experience *E* with respect to some class of tasks *T* and performance measures *P*, if its performance at tasks in *T*, as measured by *P*, improves with experience *E*." Tom Mitchell, *Machine Learning*, McGraw Hill series in Computer Sciences, New York: McGraw-Hill, 1997, quoted by Martin Thoma, "Creativity in Machine Learning", *arXiv: 1601.03642v1* [*cs.CV*] January 12, 2016.

According to a largely shared definition, "machine learning" is a branch of *artificial intelligence* based on the idea that systems can learn from data, identify patterns and make decisions with minimal human intervention. "Deep learning" is a type of *machine learning* that trains a computer to perform human-like tasks, such as recognizing speech, identifying images or making predictions. See Holger Volland, *Die kreative Macht der Maschinen*, Basel: Beltz Verlag, 2018.

15 Shlomit Yanisky-Ravid "Generating Rembrandt: Artificial Intelligence, Copyright, and Accountability in the 3d Era. The Human-Like Authors Are Already Here", 90 *Mich. St. L. Rev.* 2017, p. 659.

16 Ibid., p. 669.

> predictions about future outcomes using complex probability analysis. Like humans, deep learning programs operate with interconnected neural networks that make sense of imputed data [...]. Through a method of trial and error, deep learning programs make 'intelligent guesses' that become increasingly precise with new iterations of probability analysis.[17]

Such a wide access to all sorts of data represents a set of multiple challenges to "classic copyright regulations".[18]

So first, how does machine learning affect copyright? "Training" an algorithm may require the use of images, texts, and other data. Artworks used to feed the net can be open-source, in the public domain, or protected. While it would not be easy to determine which works have been effectively used in the training process, one wonders whether a claim for copyright infringement of protected works could be raised. Secondly, the programmer could sell the code of the algorithm as a work in itself, asking users or collectors to complete the process by generating (more or less) foreseeable outputs.

From a different, but altogether relevant, perspective, AI-generated art raises the issue of preserving algorithms;[19] their fast deprecation has encouraged some artists to qualify their output as temporary performances rather than paintings or videos.[20] Fourthly, authorship is concerned whenever an AI system, being dependent on the learning algorithm, proves to be capable of making combinations that are increasingly autonomous from the original set of materials provided by the programmer. When the deterministic nature of a piece of software turns into a probabilistic process, we observe a qualitative leap that cannot be explained by the metaphor of the "brush" or the "tool".

All these issues have legal implications that are not clearly covered by current copyright regulations. In this work I am exploring the fourth issue: its ontological nature irritates the fundamental concepts that have been used to build classic copyright law, namely authorship and originality. This is why it

---

17 Daniel Gruner and Mihaly Csikszentmihalyi, "Engineering Creativity in an Age of Artificial Intelligence", in Isabela Lebuda and Vlad Petre Glaveanu (eds.) *The Palgrave Handbook of Social Creativity Research*, Cham: Springer, 2019, p. 455.

18 When using the expression "classic copyright regulations", or "classic copyright laws", I refer to the body of enactments adopted in the course of the 19th and 20th centuries, at the level of both national and supranational law. Being "classic", these enactments are, at times, challenged by new artistic creations.

19 The business practice of recurrently updating software frameworks can make trained neural network models obsolete over time.

20 Sam Gaskin, "When Art Created by Artificial Intelligence Sells, Who Gets Paid?", *Art Market*, September 17, 2018 quoting artist Harshit Agrawal.

should be treated, I believe, as a preliminary part of a larger project aimed at making copyright laws better tuned to AI technology.

To place these technological evolutions in the context of art production, let me now introduce some examples of "AI-generated art". In 2016, a team from two Dutch museums (Mauritshuis in The Hague and Rembrandt House Museum in Amsterdam) and a research center (Technology University at Delft), sponsored by ING Bank and with the technical partnership of Microsoft, unveiled a portrait entitled *The Next Rembrandt*. It was introduced worldwide as "an artwork created by a computer"[21] that had analyzed thousands of works by the 17th-century Dutch artist Rembrandt van Rijn; an 18 month project, aimed to take on "a controversial challenge: to teach a machine to think, act and paint like Rembrandt".[22] The final 3D painting consists of more than 148 million pixels and is based on 168.263 fragments of Rembrandt's images.

One could, and in fact many did, consider this experiment nothing but a joke, or an astute form of advertising on the part of the sponsors, using new technologies and combining them with a renowned and inexpensive – being in the public domain – body of art, like that by Rembrandt van Rijn. However, even if we want to maintain a skeptical position on the artistic nature of this "experiment", we cannot deny the impact it had on new research issues in the fields of philosophy, aesthetics, ontology, and the law. Is the "New Rembrandt" a copy? It does not seem to be, as there are no originals to be copied in this case; in fact, the work has been presented as a "new painting".[23] Is it a forgery? No, for the very same reason. Perhaps a parody? Or an example of "art appropriation 4.0"?

In my view, limiting the debate on the "New Rembrandt" to the purely formal properties of an AI-produced image might lead to a dead end. Although it is the output which draws the media attention and stimulates intellectual curiosity, we should consider that this work is the result of a special generative process, composed of inputs, a learning algorithm, trained algorithms and outputs. Even if the image of a "New Rembrandt" portrait is definitively a landmark in the history of art & technology, we should keep our analysis focused on the legal issues of the *process* as a whole, from the very first step of the input, throughout the learning algorithm, the trained algorithm and, finally, the output.[24]

---

21 Mark Brown, "New Rembrandt To Be Unveiled in Amsterdam", *The Guardian*, April 5, 2016.

22 https://thenextrembrandt.pr.co/.

23 "Opinion Journal: Unveiling the Next Rembrandt", *Wall Street Journal*, August 4, 2016.

24 The definition of the four stages in the process of AI-generated art is the following:
Input, samples of existing artwork are "served" to the machine in order to train it;

Contemporary visual artists have the habit of referring to "projects", or "processes": this is one of the most remarkable traits of artists' work in the last decades. "From the mere object/artwork to the *process*" is a common saying within the conceptual artists' *milieu*. In the case of AI-generated art, thinking in terms of steps and process not only can be of support in detecting artists' intention; it also helps to understand the property issues related to these works. As will be seen in the following pages, property authorial rights on AI-generated art can be difficult to determine, due to the fact that, more or less explicitly, classic copyright law requires a human being to be the "author".

This is widely accepted worldwide, even if one cannot help quoting some different opinions:

> nowhere in the legislation or case law is there a requirement or need for there to be human thought in the Intellectual Property process or any logical reason why these rights, attaching as they do to the work generated by an AI system, created independently of the programmer or operator, could not belong to such a system.[25]

Coming back to the "New Rembrandt", we are told that the 3D reproduction technique is not only able to duplicate Rembrandt's "style", but also his use of the brushwork. However, we know that, as most great painters did in the course of their creative lives, Rembrandt van Rijn changed his perception of reality, his approach to shadows and lights, and his selection of colors over his lifetime. Can we really say that Rembrandt's *style* was duplicated by the AI?

What seems to be original, in this case, is the making of an "averaged-portrait", as a result of a machine learning analysis of all the portraits that Rembrandt painted. And this leads us to discuss what it means to introduce, thanks to technology, a statistical-based computation of the external and detectable traits of a painter, without taking into consideration other internal, perhaps unperceivable, attributes of the author's style.

Learning Algorithm, this system identifies and analyzes relevant characteristics of the Inputs, creating a data structure that forms the basis of the Trained Algorithm;

Trained Algorithm, this component uses the data structure produced by the Inputs and Learning Algorithm to create probabilities and operations that form the basis of the Outputs, or generated art;

Output, this is the result of the operations of the trained algorithm, which takes a form recognizable by the human eye as art.

For a more detailed description, see Jessica Fjeld and Mason Kortz quoted in fn. 12.

25 Colin R. Davies "An Evolutionary Step in Intellectual Property Rights. Artificial Intelligence and Intellectual Property" 27 *Computer Law & Security Rev.* 2011, 601–619, p. 610.

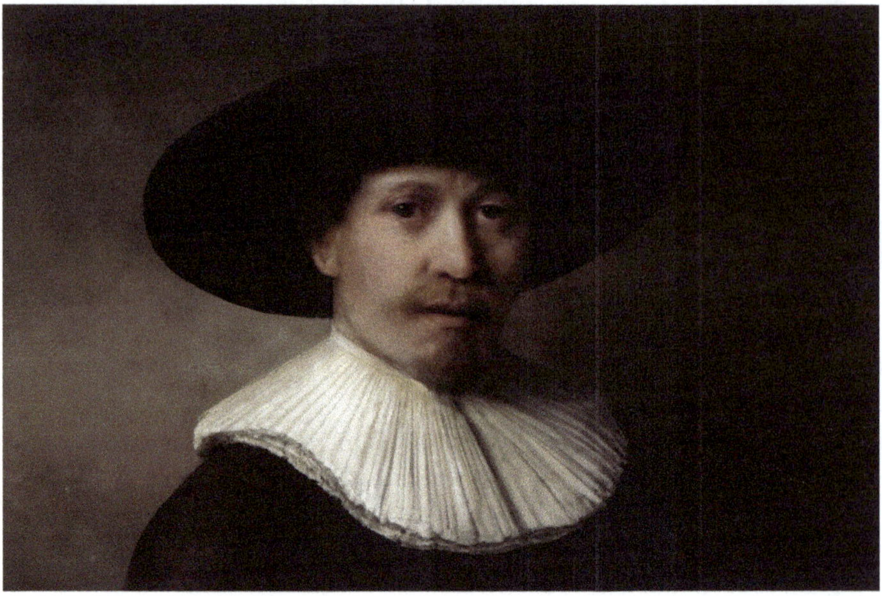

FIGURE 1 Next Rembrandt
© ING BANK / WUNDERMAN THOMPSON AMSTERDAM

In recent years, analogous experiments have been carried out also in the field of literature (a Japanese tale, "The Day A Computer Writes A Novel", qualified for a literary prize at the third Nikkei Hoshi Shinichi Literary Award).[26] Other programs have been presented as "Music composers", or "Poem writers". We can qualify these projects as mere commercial actions, pushed by the formidable investment in preparing global markets to buy automatic machineries and robots.[27] Or, we can investigate how these *oeuvres* contaminate our discourses related to digital humanities, law, philosophy, and art.

The "New Rembrandt" project does not introduce new arguments as to the authorship issue: it is pretty clear, in fact, that here technology has been used as a tool, while the artistic concept belongs to those who conceived the project. The kind of issues it raises concern aesthetical considerations, such as

26 Prof. Hitoshi Matsubara and his team (Future University Hakodate) selected the words and set the parameters before letting the AI "write" the novel autonomously. One of the team's two submissions to the competition made it past the first round of screening, despite a blind reading policy that prevents judges from knowing whether an AI was involved in the writing process; Chloe Olowitz, "A Japanese A.I. program just wrote a short novel, and it almost won a literary prize", *Digital Trends*, March 23, 2016.

27 An expansion of AI generated artwork has the potential to modify the attitudes in the art-market, as a result of the massive production of works that appear like original authorial works.

the meaning of replicating an author's style, rather than legal ones. But other elaborations in the field of AI-generated works have occurred in the last few years. These instances exploit some more radical possibilities of AI and thus produced works that are more challenging from a legal standpoint.

Computer programs have now built-in algorithms allowing them not only to learn from data input, but also to evolve and possibly make independent decisions. The Dutch case, as well as other examples in writing novels and poetry or composing songs, can be based on data learning methodologies able to generate a new, but predetermined, work, or to make "independent decisions". An important feature of this last type of AI is that, whilst programmers can set the parameters, the output is actually generated by the algorithm itself – referred to as a neural network – in a process where data representations are learned with several degrees of abstraction inspired by the functioning of the human brain.[28]

Computers are now told to be able to produce artistic or innovative outputs. These programs, however, should not be considered as either "able" or "unable" to autonomously produce works. Rather, there is a continuum linking 'computer-assisted' works on one end and autonomously generated works on the other. The middle of the continuum is broad and includes modes of creation involving varying grades of human intervention. Depending on the degree of human intervention, the form of the output may be minimally, significantly, or substantially determined by a piece of software. And while for computer-assisted works software is used as a device to produce something, for autonomously generated works the final form may be unpredictable.

How does this practice impact the legal and aesthetic discussion on creativity in the visual arts? In fact, a progression in the recourse to AI systems to generate *oeuvres* can significantly affect the art market. The world of art has its own normativity, and particularly in the case of new genres its promptness in recognizing innovation is not comparable to the capacity of copyright law to tune up with challenging issues.

According to some curators (Karthik Kalyanaraman, and his collective *64/1*, for example) and artists (Mario Klingemann, Harshit Agrawal, Memo Akten), "AI Art" has the potential to change "non-AI Art". Human artists could create new forms of painting, also as a new wave of conceptual art, to the extent that AI-generated works are comparable to a direct visualization of *instructions* or *descriptions*.

It is therefore pertinent to make reference to the appearance of photography and its impact on the art of painting:

28 See Robert Keith Sawyer, *Explaining Creativity: The Science of Human Innovation*, Oxford: OUP, 2012, 143ff.

> Aside from the much-discussed loss of the 'aura' of the artwork, and while initially painting was inspired by photography, it became more tonal at the expense of it; composition was influenced by the precise perspectives and the framing of photography. But over the longer run, by the 1880s when photography started to become accepted as a new art form, realistic precision became less valued and we also saw the loss of linear perspectival compositions, both of which photography could out-compete painting in. Suddenly the two main motors of advances in painting seemed incidental, inessential to the medium. And of course we know how radically photography and painting diverged after this.[29]

Though unpredictable, the consequences of AI on the art market can already be somewhat imagined. According to Sam Gaskin, "AI art will transform the entire Art market",[30] while Kalyanaraman believes that

> [AI] has the potential to change non-AI art as radically as the invention of photography changed painting, giving rise to Impressionism, Expressionism, and other schools more interested in the expression of uniquely human perception and emotion; [...] human artists using AI could easily create novel forms in painting and even surprising and challenging conceptual art, to the extent that such art is a direct visualization of a description. Artists whose work simply looks new (like Piet Mondrian's did), or can be described rather than felt, may see interest in their practice decline, and collectors of such works may see them lose value, the same way merely realistic images are no longer all that compelling in the age of photography.[31]

Kalyanaraman also mentions

> Mark Rothko and Paul Klee, painters that, in different ways, emphasize the experience of a work as a relationship between two sentient beings – the former by engulfing the viewer in a tsunami of fire, the latter by tickling his feet – as the sort of artists who will endure.[32]

29 Karthik Kalyanaraman, "AI Art: a New Photography Moment", https://medium.com/@info_12534/ai-art-a-new-photography moment-8d7009bfb696.

30 Sam Gaskin, quoted fn. 20.

31 Karthik Kalyanaraman, quoted fn. 29.

32 Ibid.

"Creativity machines" can be programmed in a way as to "exhibit learned skills which their creators do not possess".[33] The resulting artefacts become an epistemological case: their legal status is uncertain and depends on our attitude toward the degree of autonomy from humans that machines "enjoy".[34]

During the first decade of this century, copyright scholars' interest on the impact of AI on authorship has been flickering between understatement and overestimation, mainly due to the fact that, unlike photography or film-making, AI technology has developed intermittently and at a slow pace, in a way that was almost totally inscrutable to non-expert eyes.[35]

Quite prophetically, already in the 1990s, Sam Ricketson[36] estimated that soon the authorship of some artworks would become difficult to ascertain. He was accurate in pointing out the *absence* of human participation in the computer's output as critical with respect to the conventional notion of authorship.

Today, according to Jane Ginsburg,

> while some debate whether the human input into computer-generated outputs is in fact too attenuated to identify a human author, the burgeoning of 'computer generated works' – outputs of digital neural networks that have 'taught themselves' to combine rules of literary, musical or artistic assembly after being 'trained' on a database of pre-existing works – suggests that purely computer-generated works already exist or at least are in near prospect.[37]

---

33 Kalin Hristov, "Artificial Intelligence and the Copyright Dilemma", 57 *IDEA: The IP Law Review*, 2017, p. 434.

34 See Stephen Thaler, "Neural Networks that Autonomously Create and Discover", http://imagination-engines.com/iei_pcai.php [https://perma.cc/52TZ-GPNB] (last visited 13.01.2020).

35 On January 31, 2019, the U.S. Patent and Trademark Office (USPTO) held an event entitled: "Artificial Intelligence: Intellectual Property Considerations". On that occasion, Manny Schecter, Chief Patent Counsel at IBM, addressed one *common myth surrounding AI*, stating that "AI simply isn't there yet – AI is at the stages of augmenting and supplementing humans as a tool, sifting through large volumes of data, but not at the point where it has the ability to invent". See http://www.project-disco.org/intellectual-property/020619-views-on-ai-ip-policy-considerations-in-2019/#.XIu32VNKgfE (last visited Jan.17.01.2020).

36 Sam Ricketson, "People or Machines: The Berne Convention and the Changing Concept of Authorship", 16 *Colum. VLA J. L. & Arts* 1, 1991.

37 Jane Ginsburg, "People Not Machines: Authorship and What It Means in the Berne Convention" 49 *International Review of Intellectual Property and Competition Law*, 2018, p. 131; see also James Grimmelmann, "There's No Such Thing as a Computer-Authored Work – And It's a Good Thing, Too", 39 *Colum. J. L. & Arts*, 2016, p. 403.

In fact, what has been called "the second winter of AI"[38] (between the late 1980s and early 1990s) is now over. Also, thanks to the global and instantaneous dissemination of information on technological advances, we are now aware of the existence of programs able to compose music using "deep learning" algorithms to learn from samples of classical music.[39] Likewise, we appreciate "e-David" and "Paul," robots capable of drawing portraits in the inventive style of Patrick Tresset, their artist programmer.[40] More than just a copy machine, Tresset's robots are fitted with an "autonomous artistic creativity" that makes them capable of producing "objects that are considered as artworks".[41]

Similarly, a powerful world-wide advertising campaign informed those following contemporary art that a "generative adversarial network" (GAN),[42]

---

38 Optimism about the irrevocable progress of AI has increased since it touched a low point in the early 1990s. Since 2010 interest in AI from academic research and corporate communities has led to a renewed increase in funding and investment. It is, however, worth mentioning that for some a "new AI winter is coming soon"; see www.forbes.com/sites/cognitiveworld/2019/10/20/are-we-heading-for-another-ai-winter-soon/#5725582556d6.

39 For example, the "IAMUS" program has produced works of contemporary classical music recorded and performed by human musicians; see Sylvia Smith, "Iamus: Is this the 21st century's answer to Mozart?" BBC News (Jan. 3, 2013), http://www.bbc.com/news/technology-20889644.

Also, https://magenta.tensorflow.org/ is an open source research project exploring the role of machine learning as a tool in the creative process. While this essay is focused on contemporary visual arts, analogous considerations can be expressed as to authorship and originality requirements in the production of melodies.

40 E-David takes pictures with its camera and draws original paintings from the snapshots. By using different techniques, it makes "autonomous and unpredictable decisions about the image, the shapes and colors, the match of lights and shadows". See Shlomit Yanisky-Ravid, quoted fn. 15, p. 669.

41 See Kelly Hodgkins, "A British artist spent 10 years teaching this robot how to draw, and it totally shows", Digital Art, July 27, 2016.

42 A generative adversarial network (GAN) is a machine learning model, invented by Ian Goodfellow in 2014, in which two *neural networks* compete with each other to become more accurate in their predictions. GANs typically run unsupervised and use a cooperative zero-sum game framework to learn. The two neural networks that make-up a GAN are referred to as the generator and the discriminator. The first one is a *convolutional neural network*, while the discriminator is a *deconvolutional neural network*. The goal of the generator is to artificially manufacture outputs that could easily be mistaken for real data. The goal of the discriminator is to identify which outputs it receives have been artificially created. Basically, GANs create their own training data. As the *feedback loop* between the adversarial networks continues, the generator will begin to produce higher-quality output and the discriminator will become better at flagging data that has been artificially created.

Convolutional neural networks (CNN) consist of layers of small computational units that process visual information hierarchically in a feed-forward manner. Each layer can be understood as a collection of image filters, each of which extracts a certain feature from the input image. Therefore, the output of a given layer consists of so called "featured

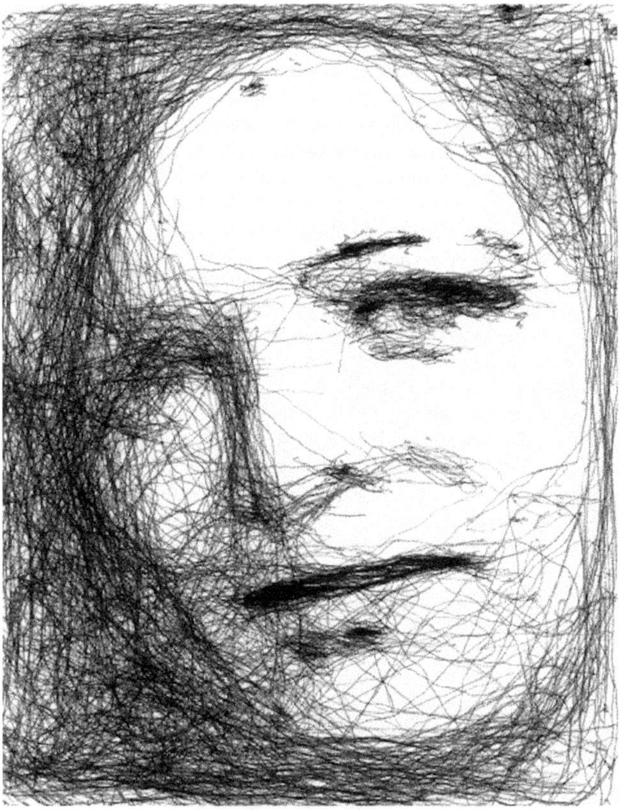

FIGURE 2 Steph by Paul-II, 2013, Ink on paper
COURTESY OF PATRICK TRESSET

having referenced 15,000 portraits from various periods, had printed a *Portrait of Edmond de Belamy* on canvas.[43] The work, signed at the bottom right with

$$\min_G \max_D E_x\left[log\left(D(x)\right)\right]+E_z\left[log\left(1-D\left(G(z)\right)\right)\right]$$

maps": differently filtered versions of the input image. The applications of convolution include *statistics, probability, computer vision, natural language processing, image* and *signal processing*.

Deconvolutional networks are convolutional neural networks that work in a reversed process. See Leon A. Gatys, Alexander S. Ecker, Matthias Bethge, "A Neural Algorithm of Artistic Style", *arXiv: 1508.06576v2* [*cs.CV*] 2 September 2015, p. 2. See also Ian J. Goodfellow, Jean Pouget-Abadie, Mehdi Mirza, Xu Bing, David Warde-Farley, Sherjil Ozair, Aaron Courville, Yoshua Bengio, "Generative Adversarial Networks", *Advances in neural information processing systems*, 2014, pp. 2672–2680.

43 "Is artificial intelligence set to become art's next medium?" www.christies.com/features/A-collaboration-between-two-artists-one-human-one-a-machine-9332-1.aspx (Last visited 14 December 2018).

namely part of the algorithm code that produced it, was presented at a Christie's auction. Expected to sell for between 7.000 and 10.000 USD, it was sold for 432.000 USD.[44]

The painting belongs to a group of eleven portraits of the imaginary Belamy family, created by a collective of artists named "Obvious" (Hugo Caselles-Dupré,

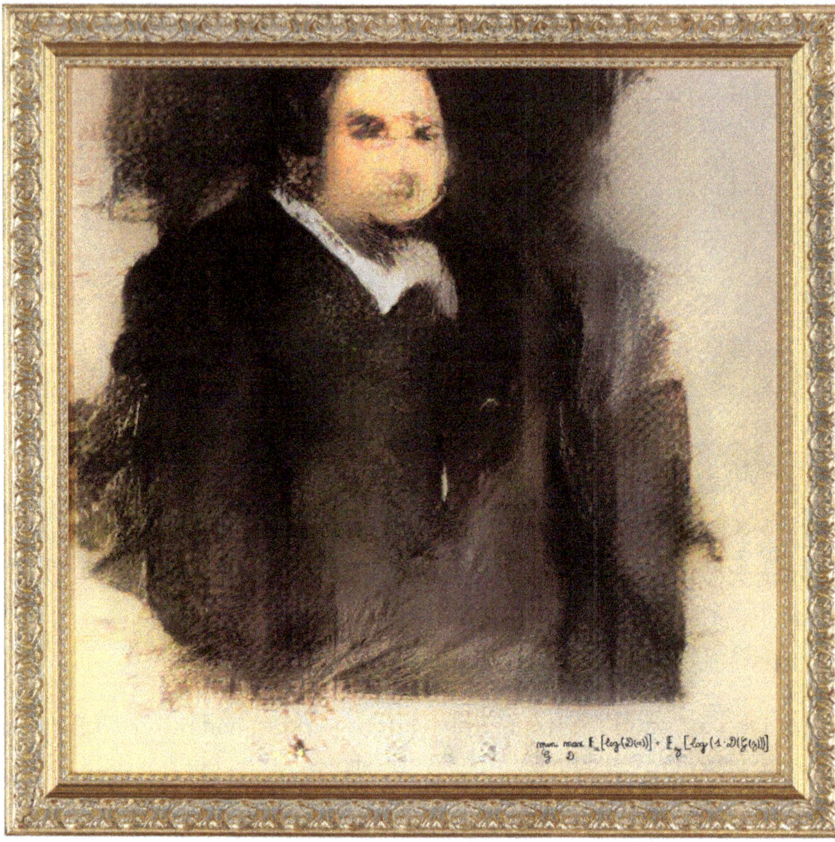

FIGURE 3 Portrait of Edmond de Belamy, 2018, created by GAN (Generative Adversarial Network)
IMAGE © OBVIOUS

44 After the sale, Massimo Sterpi noted that "the very high price is the result of a very well conducted marketing campaign, where it was presented as the first auctioned artwork of this kind: there are plenty of collectors that are looking for cutting-edge art and this was a unique opportunity for them", quoted by Louise Carronn, "Welcome to the Machine: Law, Artificial Intelligence and the Visual Arts", https://itsartlaw.org/2018/11/26/welcome-to-the-machine/.

Pierre Fautrel and Gauthier Vernier). They describe themselves as a collective of "friends, artists, and researchers, driven by a common sensibility regarding questions bounded to the increasing advent of Artificial Intelligence and Machine Learning".[45]

According to Massimo Sterpi, IP lawyer and art collector,

> *Portrait of Edmond de Belamy* is embedding all the current doubts and issues of algorithmic art: it is not even clear if it is protected by copyright (is its human element enough?) and, in the affirmative, who owns such copyright.[46]

"Obvious" is engaged in exploring the interface between art and artificial intelligence, and their method has been clearly spelt out in a *Manifesto*:

> *Art: a perfect land of experiment*
> Art is a perfect medium that allows to experiment with the possibilities of an AI and better understand how it all works. Here are four art features we identified as being helpful in our research.
> – *Art is tangible*: it offers some concrete results.
> – *It is accessible*: most people have an affinity with some kind of art.
> – *Art is interpretable*: it offers another way to experiment and leads to debates that are at least as interesting as the answers you can get by the purely scientific field.
> – *Art is free*, and it cannot be restrained by our own creativity when experiencing with it.
>
> Therefore, art seemed like the perfect way to experiment with creativity as expressed by artificial intelligence.
>
> When talking about art, we consider all types of applications that we start to see appearing around us. Music made by a *collaboration between human and machines*, poems, scripts, lyrics, trailers, and images made by algorithms. All *these projects have in common the replacement of part of the creativity process*. Each one of them is different in the level of human intervention it involves. We can say that once the whole process will have been automated, we will have created a machine that is capable of being

45 www.obvious-art.com.

46 Quoted by Louise Carron, "Welcome to the Machine: Law, Artificial Intelligence and the Visual Arts", https://itsartlaw.org/2018/11/26/welcome-to-the-machine/.

> creative, in the same way a human is. Nevertheless, it has not been done yet.[47] [emphasis added]

As a matter of fact, the *Paul*-originated paintings have been exhibited in major art museums and have been acquired by galleries, museums, and art fairs for display. The Belamy portrait has been sold at Christie's. These examples, among others, make it evident that questioning the nature of an artwork produced by automatic systems is not a pursuit confined within a pure theoretical debate.[48]

The existence of these works, and in particular, their appearance in the art world, force us to understand their place within the space of copyright regulation, as well as within the art world. This urges us to delineate legal relationships among human ideas, human users, and machine-generated expressions. Also, it drives us to define an essential element of copyright: creativity. This is not to say that AI has replaced the human artist. At least, in the understanding of the "*Obvious*" collective, the parties should remain clearly separated:

> If you ask me: 'Will AI be the artist of tomorrow', I would be tempted to answer: 'Is the camera the artist of today?' It is not. AI is a new tool, allowing the maximization of the creative potential of humans. Nevertheless, for the first time, humans also have the possibility of maximizing the creative potential of their tool.[49]

However, some important actors from the art world play with the categories of creativity; introducing *Portrait of Edmond de Belamy* at an auction, Christie's site reports:

> This portrait is not the product of a human mind. It was created by an artificial intelligence, an algorithm defined by that algebraic formula with its many parentheses.[50]

---

47 Obvious – Artificial Intelligence for Art – Manifesto www.obvious-art.com; "We found that portraits provided the best way to illustrate our point, which is that algorithms are able to emulate creativity" Hugo Caselles-Dupré, quote from www.obvious-art.com.

48 Already four centuries ago, even before Descartes opened a new perspective to philosophical investigation on the relationships between technology, ontology, and free will, academics supported "interdisciplinary" debates on the nature of "*Automata*" animated by magnets. See Derek J. de Solla Price, "Automata and the Origins of Mechanism and Mechanistic Philosophy" 5 *Technology and Culture*, 1964, 9–23, p. 23.

49 https://medium.com/@hello.obvious/a-naive-yet-educated-perspective-on-art-and-artificial-intelligence-9e16783e73da.

50 Ibid.

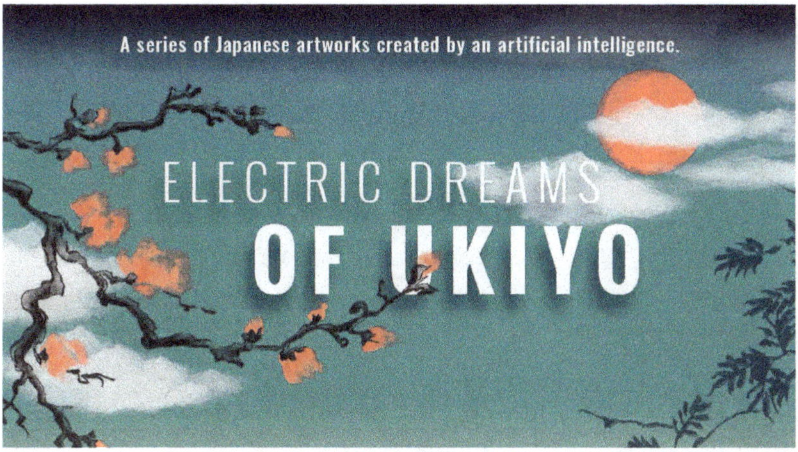

FIGURE 4 Electric Dreams of Ukiyo. A series of Japanese artworks created by an artificial intelligence.
© IMAGE OBVIOUS

And, in a different project, named "Electric Dreams of Ukiyo. A Series of Japanese Artworks Created by an Artificial Intelligence",[51] the same authors' collective emphasized the role of AI in *creating*, through a GAN system, the images. In the meantime, the art world has already welcomed these works, and priced the images around 10.000 euros at recent auctions.

What we can learn from these works is the following: artists keen to challenge the limits of authorship engage in technology. And even when they remain vague about paternity (*Obvious* artists do not claim that the AI is the author, but at the same time the portraits are signed with an algorithm), the art world (in this case, Christie's auction house) plays its role in attracting these new *oeuvres* within the precincts of recognized art.

Many cases such as the "New Rembrandt" have put AI art under the spotlight. The most interesting ones are the following.

In the press materials circulated to introduce "Gradient Descent", an exhibition held at the *Nature Morte* New Delhi gallery from August 17 to September 15 2018, the curators stated:

> The exhibit presents works created entirely by artificial intelligence in collaboration with Harshit Agrawal, Memo Akten, Jake Elwes, Mario Klingemann, Anna Ridler, Nao Tokui & Tom White. Gradient Descent is

---

51 Ibid.

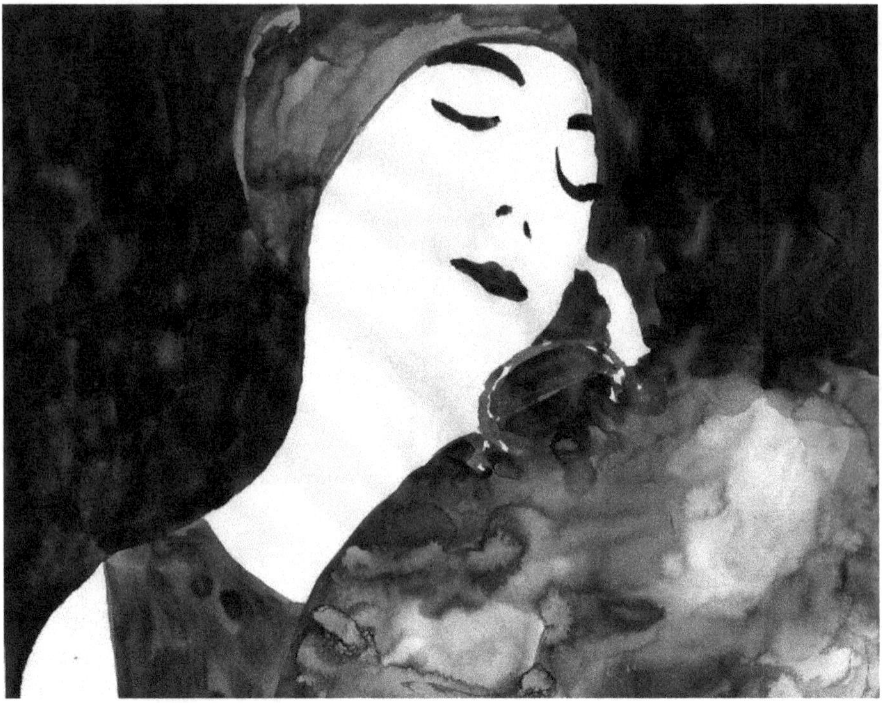

FIGURE 5 From the series "Fall of House of Ushers"
COURTESY OF ANNA RIDLER

the first ever art exhibition in India to include artwork made entirely by artificial intelligence.[52]

AIart seems interesting because it looks convincing: beautiful and creative. Its works possess aesthetic value in more or less the traditional sense. Knowing that they are outcomes of AI can change our perception to some extent, much like knowing that a Renaissance palace has been reconstructed after the war can change our appreciation of its nature. Still, in both cases we preserve our aesthetic appreciation: a weakened authorship (in the case of AI), or a feebler originality (in the case of a reconstructed ancient building) do not necessarily invalidate our aesthetic judgement. What they do trouble, instead, is the law: in particular, lack of recognizable human authorship can lead to absence of legal protection. as I will show later on in this essay.

With or without the full recognition of the legal world, however, the art world has welcomed AI "made" works. Whether it is called automatic painting

52 Sam Gaskin quoted fn. 19, p. 3. As known, "gradient descent" is also one of the most popular optimization algorithms used in machine learning.

or a renewed form of conceptual art,[53] either way, we are seeing its appearance in the debate on authorship and creativity:

> Since the inception of Google's DeepDream in 2015, an algorithm devised to visualize data representations of neural networks and the creation of tools for image-to-image translation, there has been an explosion of artists working with artificial intelligence to create artworks that address the very foundation of visual art: visual creativity. Unlike traditional technology-driven artworks in which artists utilized technology as a tool for their own creative vision, AI Art takes into account not only the artist's vision, but the machine's as well; thus allowing the machine to become a peer and collaborator in this process for the very first time.[54]

AI-generated art is looking for its place in the art market. Aparajita Jain, co-director of the mentioned *Nature Morte* gallery, said she priced the works in the *Gradient Descent* exhibition "quite aggressively, and up to $40,000, to help establish AI art as a *genre*".[55]

There is an innovative facet, which brands AI-made art as distinctive from a simple recourse to technology-produced images. As emphasized by the curators of the *Gradient Descent* project, the key aspect is a new "collaboration" between the human being and the machine, which sweeps over the traditional concept of "an artist using a tool":

> This group of artists, utilizing unique and innovative practices, question this form of art making and the ownership of the creative vision. While the visual side of the creative task is now shifted to an algorithm – a machine – the machine can only create works based on its own experience and its exposure to visual languages. It is here, in the art of teaching the machine and in designing the humanly interpretable concept of the artwork, that the locus of the human's creativity lies within this genre [...]. Like every important paradigm shift in the history of art and art making before it, AI Art challenges us to rethink what art is and how it is made.[56]

53 "If you consider the whole process, then what you have is something more like conceptual art than traditional painting" stated Ahmed Elgammal, director of the Art and Artificial Intelligence Laboratory at Rutgers University Ahmed Elgammal, quoted in www.christies.com/features/A-collaboration-between-two-artists-one-human-one-a-machine-9332-1.aspx (last visited May 31, 2020).

54 http://naturemorte.com/exhibitions/gradientdescent/ (last visited February 28, 2020).

55 Sam Gaskin, quoted fn. 20, p. 4.

56 http://naturemorte.com/exhibitions/gradientdescent/ (last visited February 28, 2020).

Art history shows that every now and then musicians like Schoenberg, painters like Malevič, or writers like Joyce pierce the veil of tradition, reversing the canon and conceiving new ways and forms to express their art. What they design and produce remains over the centuries; their artworks are the big waves, overturning the waters of traditional art. Quite often great masters emerge from difficult times, marked by wide-ranging lack of interest towards their work. Other times, their aesthetic revolution succeeds from the first very moment.

Anyhow, whether in a timely or belated fashion, the public is the ultimate judge of their unconventional production. "Unconventional" is the proper word here, meaning the aptitude to deviate from the conventional canons of visual arts. Innovative art often uses contra-standard categorical properties. Sometimes we have examples that are so unconventional that they require establishing a new category.[57] But can AI-generated art be unconventional?

In fact, it is one thing to reproduce a painting resulting from the digestion of thousands of similar artworks, but it is a different matter to produce works marked by a new "style". As mentioned, the production of an "average portrait", resulting from quantitative measurements of the traits employed by an artist, does not seem to be, *per se*, a satisfactory example of an unconventional painting. Technological innovation does not necessarily include artistic innovation.

To advance into the field of originality, via the implementation of GAN systems, Ahmed Elgammal, director of the Art and Artificial Intelligence Laboratories at Rutgers University in New Jersey, has modified a generative adversarial network and worked out a system called CAN (Creative Adversarial Network): a "creative" rather than a "generative" network. The system is specifically programmed to produce images different from the ones received, which in this case consists of works attributed to all styles in painting from the 14th century onwards.

Like other works mentioned in these pages, the ones produced through a CAN system have received appreciation by the art world. Big auction houses have warmed the attention of collectors, introducing these *oeuvres* into the world of visual art. For those who embrace an institutional theory of art, these works are thus fully legitimate, having been "baptized" by artwork institutions as genuine – if not good – art.

---

57 In "Categories of Art," Kendall Walton discusses how things like genres influence our perception of an artwork's standard, neutral, and contra-standard properties. *The Philosophical Review*, No. 3, 1970, pp. 334–367; I thank Andrea Baldini for this reference.

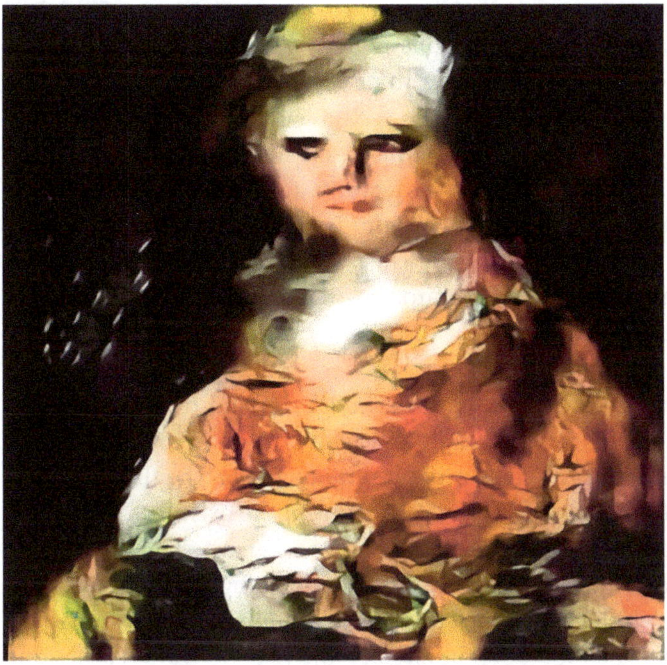

FIGURE 6 AICAN Faceless Portrait # Creative adversarial network print on canvas. 2019
COURTESY OF AHMED ELGAMMAL

This last case stretches to its extremes the innovative capacity of AI-made works to depart from established canons and produce *oeuvres* that are not foreseeable by those who designed the algorithms.

Later I will address the issue of the legal definition of creativity for the purpose of copyright laws. As to the philosophical definition, its density goes beyond the scope of this essay. Clearly enough, AI art stimulates further reflections on the links between *internal* and *external* creativity or, as Boden contends, between psychological and historical creativity.[58] AI art may very well never be psychologically creative. But perhaps it could be historically creative.

The machine is not, obviously, departing from traditional canons thanks to "its" artistic capacity to "feel" the urge of a new canon. We are, however, facing an emulation of creativity which, in itself, is a different phenomenon than pure imitation. It is an emulation capable of leaving a mark in the history of visual arts.

58 Boden Margaret, *The Creative Mind: Myths and Mechanisms*, Routledge: New York, 2004.

Take abstraction, for example.[59] Abstract canvas emerged as an original wave of painting – a vast new field, unconstrained by the canon of naturalism.

According to its developers, CAN algorithms

> produce abstract images, because the algorithm has grasped that art progresses in a certain trajectory. If it wants to make something novel, then it cannot go back and produce figurative works as existed before the 20th century it has to move forward. The network has learned that it finds more solutions when it tends towards abstraction: that is where there is the space for novelty.

One algorithm creates a solution, the other judges it, and the system loops back and forth until the intended result is reached.[60] The innovative aspect, here, is that the generator is told to produce an image that the discriminator recognizes as "art", but which does not fall into any of the existing styles.

If humans are not the ones triggering the action taken by an automatic system, nor the ones placed at the end of the process supplying sufficient "intellectual creation" to match the minimum standard of authorship requested by the Berne Convention for the Protection of Literary and Artistic Works (UCB), one might well consider these outputs to be "autonomously computer-generated".

The UCB[61] rests upon two main principles:

---

59 See Werner Gephart, "Abstraction: A Myth of the Occidental World", Werner Gephart and Jure Leko (eds.), *Law and the Arts. Elective Affinities and Relationships of Tension*, Frankfurt a./M.: Klostermann, 2017, pp. 291–313.

60 The idea is to make art that is "novel, but not too novel", says Marian Mazzone, an art historian at the College of Charleston in South Carolina who worked on the project. See www.newscientist.com/article/2139184-artificially-intelligent-painters-invent-new-styles-of-art/#ixzz6DIGGzbuP.

Once the AI had produced a series of images, members of the public were asked to judge them alongside paintings made by people in an online survey, without knowing which were which. Participants answered questions about how complex or novel they felt each image was, and whether it inspired them or elevated their mood. To the researchers' surprise, images produced by the AI often scored slightly higher than those made by humans.

61 At the international level, copyright legislation does not cover AI artefacts.

A general list of applicable International and EU sources of law related to Copyright and Intellectual Property includes the following:

- Agreement on Trade-Related Aspects of Intellectual Property Rights (TRIPS);
- Berne Convention for the Protection of Literary and Artistic Works (UBC);
- UNESCO Universal Copyright Convention (UCC);
- WIPO Copyright Treaty (WCT);

- the first one, derived from the French original regulation of "*les Droits de l'Auteur*", enables the author to hold a bundle of exclusive rights, centered on their personality;
- the second one (often considered as part of the "spirit" of the common law) is based on utilitarian reasons to justify authorial privileges as exceptional, the justification being that, with no protection for authors' property rights, desirable works would not be produced.

UCB drafters repeatedly employed the term "author" throughout the text, but they never provided a clear definition of it. Most commentators believe that the Convention implicitly requires an author to be human. Following Sam Ricketson, for instance, the notion of a human creator as the foundation for authorship can be retrieved from several articles of the UCB, such as: the period of protection given to authors, which is contingent to the author's life, or the protection of moral rights, which only makes sense in relation to a human author. Other scholars[62] argue that the UCB does not necessarily require human authorship for a work to be granted copyright protection, noting that the Convention does not exclude legal entities from copyright protection, and thus acknowledging a relevant exception to the principle of purely human authorship.

As we know, international regulations on copyrights, in spite of their search for a "universal character", have been strongly influenced by the 19th century styled European continental theories on authorship. A different historical and political context led the U.S. common law to consider mainly the output of the process – the artefact. Instead, the French-based doctrine and consequent

---

- Directive 93/83/EEC on the coordination of certain rules concerning copyright and rights related to copyright applicable to satellite broadcasting and cable retransmission;
- Directive 96/9/EC on the legal protection of databases;
- Directive 2001/29/EC on the harmonization of certain aspects of copyright and related rights in the information society;
- Directive 2004/48/EC on the enforcement of intellectual property rights;
- Directive 2011/77/EU amending Directive 2006/116/EC on the term of protection of copyright and certain related rights;
- Directive 2006/116/EC on the term of protection of copyright and certain related rights;
- Directive 2009/24/EC on the legal protection of computer programs.

See also WIPO (2019). *WIPO Technology Trends 2019: Artificial Intelligence*. Geneva: World Intellectual Property Organization, Geneva.

62 See Enrico Bonadio and Nicola Lucchi (eds.), "*Non-Conventional Copyright. Do New and Non-Traditional Works Deserve Protection?*" Elgar: London, 2018; Anniina Huttunen and Anna Ronkainen, "Translation Technology and Copyright" *Nordic Intellectual Property Review* (2012), pp. 330–344.

regulations adopted in continental Europe focused on the author, a free and creative person, citizen of the enlightened society, able to transfer their temperament into an artistic endeavor. This diversity between the two major legal systems of the world – even if softened since the 1990s, when some U.S. Federal regulations intervened to provide a certain protection to visual art authors[63] – has not completely disappeared, so that we can still consider the European continental legislations as being more inclined to protect artists' rights, while the U.S. law remains somehow focused on the results of the artistic process.

Let us assume, then, that an *oeuvre* is produced via an independent AI process, free from human intervention in the making; what would its legal status be? According to most authors, copyright law is not currently structured to accommodate the innovative authorship frame of "people-who-write-programs-that-make-art".[64] This position can be read in two different ways: the first one, innovative, would lead to urge the recognition of authorship to programs-that-make-art; the second one, conservative, would maintain that copyright laws only cover "human authorial rights". To fill the gap, therefore, one should resort to a legal fiction arguing that, for example, only the collective "Obvious" could have painted the images composed by the CAN algorithms.

However, the latest generation AI-operated systems have made it difficult to understand where the programmer's contribution ends and the user's role begins. This becomes even more confusing when the program is coded to produce expressive choices independently of both programmer and user. Is, then, the challenge brought by AI to copyright law so robust as to suggest a change of perspective on the requirements of authorship?

This query does, unquestionably, irritate classic copyright law, whose structure is centered on the author. However, we should not forget the lesson taught by the history of visual arts: for centuries it was the work, rather than the author, that was at the center of the stage. This paradigm changed to the point of reversing its direction, from the object/artwork towards the subject/artist, only with the advent of the romantic idea of authorship and, later on, with the omnipotence of the authorial act (Duchamp, Man Ray). Once the classic canon had been broken, visual arts embraced a variety of movements throughout the 20th century. Some highlighted the subjective/authorial side, to the point of defining *what* art is by looking at *who* makes indecipherable works. Others

63 The *Visual Artists Rights Act* of 1990 (VARA), was the first Federal *copyright* legislation to grant protection to authors' *moral rights*.

64 See Lior Zemer, "Rethinking Copyright Alternatives", 14 *International Journal of Law and Information Technology*, 2006, pp. 137–145, https://doi.org/10.1093/ijlit/eai024; see also Lior Zemer, *The Idea of Authorship in Copyright*, London: Routledge, 2016.

stressed that a work of art could only result from a *process* to be completed by the viewer.[65]

So far, copyright laws within common law countries have proven to be loose enough to cover many of those cases; this happened, however, at the cost of increased litigation. As ever, indeterminacy in the current law ends up in uncertainties of adjudication.[66] In Europe, there have been no actions for a unitary strategy, as heterogeneity and slowness in adapting regulations are caused by legal diversities and normative traditions in different countries. In fact, the regulation of intellectual property and copyright was left to the legislative competence of the Member States: the Treaty of Rome establishing the European Community (1957) did not intend to regulate property rights related to creations or inventions. Accordingly, its art. 222 indicated: "This Treaty does not in any way prejudice the rules of the property regime in Member States".[67]

However, creative actions and the dissemination of artworks tend to surpass national borders. That is why it seemed necessary to partially overcome the competence issue, to ensure that intellectual property enjoys an equivalent

65 Gonzalez-Torres, for example, wanted his work to be disseminated; he believed that it was not fully accomplished without the participation of the viewer: "Without the public these works are nothing. I ask the public to help me, to take responsibility, to become part of my work, to join in". www.theartstory.org/artist/gonzalez-torres-felix/.

To understand public participation in art-making in the context of the theories of the ontology art one should refer to the phenomenology of Roman Ingarden (see Bohdan Dziemidok and Peter McCornick eds., *On the Aesthetics of Roman Ingarden: Interpretations and Assessments*, Kluwer: The Hague, 1989) and to the imputationalism of Michael Krausz (see his *Rightness and Reasons: Interpretation in Cultural Practices*, Cornell Univ. Press: Ithaca, 1993). In the literature on public art, this view is widespread. See Andrea Baldini, "Identity and Interpretation of Public Artworks: A Challenge to Intentionalism.", in 8 *Kultura-Społeczeństwo-Edukacja*, 2015, pp. 9–26.

66 On February 2020 the Art & Law Litigation Conference held by the Federal Bar Association in New York had a panel devoted to "The Business of Robo-Art: How AI is Changing the Way Physical and Digital Art is Created, Traded and Collected"; the panelists included John Cahill, Ahmed Elgammal, Luke Nikas, and Massimo Sterpi.

67 Today, at the level of primary legislation, EU Treaties deal with copyright only as to the obligation for the EU to create an operational environment for copyright protection (Treaty on the Functioning of the European Union, arts. 118, 207 and 262). Within secondary legislation, the *Computer Programs Directive* (2009/24) grants protection to software "If it is original in the sense that it is the author's own intellectual creation" (art. 1.3). See Luigi Carlo Ubertazzi "IP and the Draft Treaty on the EU", 38 *IIC – Int. R. IP & Comp. L.* (2007), 881; Marco Ricolfi, "Towards an EU Copyright Code? A Conceptual Framework", Irina Stamatoudi (ed.) *New Developments in EU and International Copyright Law*, Kluwer: New York, 2016, Ch. 18.

level of protection in the internal market.[68] Even if still partial, this is the aim of many EU Directives adopted in the last 20 years. Nevertheless, in spite of a number of Position Papers, White Books, Governmental Reports and Recommendations,[69] national lawmakers have not yet tackled the subject. To most policymakers the matter seems still unripe; in their opinion, existing copyright laws can respond, at both national[70] and international level, to the challenges brought by AI-generated artworks.[71]

---

68 In my opinion point 18 of the quoted (fn. 1) European Parliament resolution dated 16 February 2017 is too vague, if not wrong, when it notes "*that there are no legal provisions that specifically apply to robotics, but that existing legal regimes and doctrines can be readily applied to robotics*, although some aspects appear to call for specific consideration" [emphasis added].

69 See, e.g.: "La Stratégie France I.A: soutenir la dynamique française autour de l'intelligence artificielle" (20.01.2017) adopted by the French Ministère de l'enseignement supérieur, de la recherche et de l'innovation; the recommendations to the EU Commission already quoted *supra* at fn. 1; in the UK, the report "Robotics and Artificial Intelligence" (13.09.2016), adopted by the Science and Technology Committee of the House of Commons; or, in the US, the Report and Recommendations "Preparing for the future of AI", published in October 2016 by the National Science and Technology Council-Subcommittee on Machine Learning and Artificial Intelligence.

70 As is often the case when the enacted law is no longer in tune with technological or societal progress, judges are left to decide whether and how to reconcile outdated regulations with new technologies. Already in the early 1980s, for example, disputes arose concerning copyrights in electronic video games and their audio-visual displays. In those cases, some judges held that game displays were copyrightable by the holder of the copyright in the game program that generated the displays. Moreover, the courts said, it doesn't matter whether the displays were generated autonomously by the machine, or through the actions of a player during the game's "play" mode. In either case, the display was ruled to be copyrightable, and the copyright belonging to the owner of the copyright in the game code. See "Atari, Inc. v. North American Philips Consumer Elec. Corp.", 672 F.2d 607, 610 (7th Cir. 1982); "Williams Elec., Inc. v. Artic Int'l., Inc.", No. 81–1852, 1981 U.S. Dist.

In the English case *Nova Productions vs. Mazooma Games* [2007] EWCA Civ 219, the Court of Appeal had to decide on the authorship of a computer game and declared that a player's input "is not artistic in nature and he has contributed no skill or labour of an artistic kind".

71 According to Hristov: "over the last two hundred years, a number of amendments have been made to the U.S. copyright law to accommodate for changes in societal norms. With the rapid growth in speed and capability of modern computers, artificial intelligence has secured a more prominent position as a driver of innovation. Little has been done, however, to accommodate for this fact". Kalin Hristov, "Artificial Intelligence and the Copyright Survey", JSPG, Vol. 16, Issue 1, April 2020, p. 21 www.researchgate.net/publication/337387886_Artificial_Intelligence_and_the_Copyright_Survey/citation/download.

Earlier, in 1974, the formation of the Commission of New Technological Uses of Copyrighted Works (CONTU) by the U.S. Congress was meant to address regulatory issues related to the new emerging technologies and the rapid growth of personal computers

In my view, this position holds as long as one maintains that artworks produced by machines are *derived* from human action. Until recently, in fact, it was common belief that a machine, though defined as "intelligent", lacked "creative aptitude" to produce artworks:[72] as is well known, the law in many countries only protects "original" works created by human intelligence.[73]

"Until recently", I said – today many new projects attest that it is worth not dismissing the matter as simply irrelevant. A prophecy expressed by Paul Valéry almost a century ago, and later expanded by Walter Benjamin, is proving true:

> We must expect great innovations to transform the entire technique of the arts, thereby affecting artistic invention itself and perhaps even bringing about an amazing change in our very notion of art.[74]

3 Kaleidoscope: Authors and Artworks between Classic Law and the Art World[75]

Should we consider an AI system as an independent maker of an *oeuvre*, we would still be far from solving a further issue: authorship. From what was said until now, traditional copyright law seems to have accepted either one or the other of these two mutually exclusive disjuncts: artificial intelligence is

---

use in the U.S. The Commission, asked to articulate recommendations for the Congress on copyright in the computer age, declared in its 1978 report that computers were *simply tools whose main function was to assist human authors in the creative process* [emphasis added]. In addition, the report also stated that independently generated computer works required no particular consideration since autonomous works were not deemed possible in the foreseeable future. See *National Commission on New Technological Uses of Copyrighted Works. Final Report.* http://eric.ed.gov/PDFS/ED160122.pdf.

72 James Grimmelmann, quoted fn. 36, commenting on the "Next Rembrandt" portrait, said that the work "involves a great deal of sophisticated computer programming, but it is essentially a mash-up produced through persistent human supervision and direction of the inputs".

73 As early as 1965 the Register of Copyrights expressed concern about whether a computer could own rights in computer-generated works; see *U.S. Copyright Office, 68th Annual Report of the Register of Copyrights*.

74 Paul Valéry, *Pièces Sur L'art. La Conquête de l'ubiquité* (1928), quoted by Walter Benjamin as the epigraph to his *The Work of Art in the Age of Mechanical Reproduction*, 1935.

75 The term was introduced by Arthur Danto in his celebrated article "The Artworld", in 61 *The Journal of Philosophy*, 1964, pp. 571–584. It is a wider term than *art market*; Becker defines it as "the network of people whose cooperative activity, organized via their joint knowledge of conventional means of doing things, produce(s) the kind of art works that the art world is noted for". See Howard Samuel Becker, *Art Worlds*, Berkeley: University of California Press, 1982.

a mystical author or an insensitive machine. Neither solution, however, fully captures the most recent instances of interaction between humans and machines. This is why, to articulate a normative[76] discourse consistent with what is currently happening in the art world, we should also look outside of the perimeter of classical copyright law.

To be sure, amendments have been made to update the 135-years-old text of the Bern Convention, and national copyright laws have been repeatedly adjusted to technological innovations. What has not been modified, in spite of the revolutionary transformation of visual arts that occurred in the last one hundred years, is the core of the regulatory scheme, which is based on property law.

Regardless of national choices, all copyright regulations derive from property law, and their diversities can be explained by looking at the past origins of property legal regimes. To play its role, property law requires classifications, so that everyone can recognize what is included within its range of protection. We call this area the static\protective role of property law.

Historically, property law has been about protecting tangible objects like lands, chattels, assets. Later on, the protection of immaterial interests was brought within the scope of property law. A good functioning property law identifies the person to whom rights can be entitled. A second classification then appears, listing the possible holders of property rights. Being part of this classification entails relevant economic consequences: you can buy, trade, use and (sometimes) even peruse the owned object. We call this area the dynamic\functional role of property law.

Both roles assigned to property law are sustained by a set of taxonomies, aimed to deploy the potential "who" (*subject*) and the suitable "what" (*object*). For ages, lawmakers and judges did not feel the need to define these roles in the case of artistic creations. The law had rarely to deal with disputes arising in the art world, nor was there a particular necessity to define "who" was an artist, or "what" their action was about. Several enactments, both at the international and national levels, mentioned non-exhaustive lists of objects to be considered artworks, such as for example: "works of drawing, painting, architecture, sculpture, engraving and lithography; photographic works" (Berne Convention, Art. 2.1), without indulging in qualifications, and simply leaving it to judges to apply the law on a case-by-case basis.

As long as artists remained loyal to the classifications and genres, this method proved to be fairly efficient: judges, while interpreting the classic copyright law, could focus on the physical expressions through which visual works were

76 In this essay I intend *normative* as *legal*.

normally made visible, and on the processes which typically assigned physical works to the genre classifications. In so doing, they could refrain from investigating the aesthetic value of a contended object.

Everything changed at the turn of the 20th century when, *because* of artists' innovations (dada, ready-made, surrealism), law practitioners, and particularly judges, began to be often puzzled. They were about to lose the deep-rooted set of references they had used to qualify artworks (objects) and to define artists (subjects). In fact, the qualification of the artistic object turned out to be problematic as the two worlds (the world of law and the art world) split up. More precisely, the art world pulled away, while the world of law continued along a traditional path, where works are made by the hand of the artist, the genres are clearly identified, and the material for a sculpture is solid like stone and bronze.

Facing all these correspondences between property and copyright regulations, why, then, should one treat the latter as a separate field of the law? A response to this question was neatly formulated by Immanuel Kant:

> On the one hand, a book is a corporeal artefact [...] that can be reproduced (by someone in legitimate possession of a copy of it), so that there is a right to a thing with regard to it. On the other hand, a book is also a mere discourse of the publisher to the public, which the publisher may not repeat publicly without having a mandate from the author to do so [...] and this is a right against a person. The error consists in mistaking one of these rights for the other.[77]

Since then, and over the following hundred years, the articulation of copyright laws was centered on the clear identification of works of art as things that could be separated from the set of ordinary items because of some special intangible feature they had.

Almost at the same time as Kant was active, during the second half of the 18th century, on the two sides of the Atlantic policymakers were enacting statutes and regulations whose aim was to give protection and incentives to "learned and ingenious persons".[78] A recurrent characterization of North American and French post-revolutionary legislation has emphasized

77 *The Metaphysics of Moral* (1797). Quoted by Tiziana Andina, "What is Art? The Question of Definition Reloaded", 1.2 *Art and Law*, New York, Dordrecht: Brill, 2017, p. 13.

78 Preamble of the Massachusetts Copyright Act, the first general copyright statute to be enacted in the American states. (An Act for the purpose of securing to authors the exclusive right and benefit of publishing their literary productions for twenty-one years, 1783, Mass. Acts 369).

dissimilarities between the two legal patterns, the first more focused on the utilitarian value of arts and science,[79] the second said to "enshrine the author".[80] Both political orders, however, originated from a revolutionary break against *Anciens régimes*, and were a cradle for theories unveiling the social impact of the law on economic growth.

Whether the diversity between the French and the U.S. copyright regulations has been overstated[81] or not, the common feeling portrayed revolutionary French law as the best shield for artists, also thanks to the perception of the "existence of an intimate and almost sacred bond between authors and their works as the source of a strong literary and artistic property right".[82] This bond was due to the articulation of authors' non-economic rights as irrevocable and permanent "*Droits de la personalité*". This outlived the 20th century to support the idea of "(only) human creativity". Unlike U.S. early copyright legislation, then, French copyright law extended not merely to "writings of all kinds" but to "all productions of the *beaux arts*". Accordingly, the different philosophical conceptions underpinning the U.S. and the European continental copyright regulations resulted in different classifications of artworks: promoting "utility"

Copyright Statutes that created general copyright regimes on the state level were passed in 12 out of 13 of the States between 1783 and 1786. The States' copyright Acts were the result of local lobbying by various authors and their political allies, as well as of a resolution by the Continental Congress recommending such state legislation. They mark a rising interest in the United States in copyright protection and an ideological reorientation from favor for the public domain (based on a strong political dislike of private monopolies) toward authors' rights and interests.

79 See Anthony Julius, Malcolm Quinn, Philip Schofield (eds.), *Bentham and the Arts*, UCL Press: London, 2020.

80 According to Jane Ginsburg ("A Tale of Two Copyrights: Literary Property in Revolutionary France and America", 64 *Tul. L. Rev.* 1990, p. 99) "the examination of the French revolutionary sources of copyright laws reveals that legislators, courts, and advocates perceived literary property primarily as a means to advance public instruction. Contemporary authorities certainly also recognized authors' claims of personal rights arising out of their creations, but the characteristic portrayal of French revolutionary copyright as an unambiguous espousal of an author-centric view of copyright requires substantial amendment", p. 1023.

81 "[The] familiar conceptions of early U.S. copyright also warrant reconsideration. If U.S. copyright's exponents sought to promote the progress of knowledge, they also recognized that the author's labors are due their own reward. The revolutionary French and American systems shared much not only in theory, but also in practice" Jane C. Ginsburg, quoted, fn. 79 p. 992.

82 Ibidem, p. 993.

meant focusing on useful works (like charts, maps, books), while including *beaux arts* meant, under French law, protecting also music, drama, novels.[83]

Why this reminder of the contingency of taxonomies in law and art? Let me explain. To grasp social reality, lawyers need to frame it within schemes and lists. Copyright regulations share with other fields of law, such as property law[84] (lists of owners' prerogatives and categories of goods) and constitutional law (list of fundamental rights), a longing for classifications. Normally, social reality stretches over classifications and this leads national legal orders either to opt for open lists thus converting normative catalogs into exemplary inventories – or to make adjustments. These strategies, in turn, increase worldwide diversities in regulations. This is why the adoption of a uniform legislation was marked by the recognition of an excess of diversity in what had to be protected by copyright.

Let's consider art. 2.1. (UCB, 1886):

> The expression "literary and artistic works" shall include every production in the literary, scientific and artistic domain, *whatever may be the mode or form of its expression*, such as books, pamphlets and other writings; lectures, addresses, sermons and other works of the same nature; dramatic or dramatic-musical works; choreographic works and entertainments in dumb show; musical compositions with or without words; *cinematographic works to which are assimilated works expressed by a process analogous to cinematography*; works of drawing, painting, architecture, sculpture, engraving and lithography; photographic works to which are assimilated works expressed by a process analogous to photography; works of applied art; illustrations, maps, plans, sketches and three-dimensional works relative to geography, topography, architecture or science. [emphasis added]

The Berne catalogue espouses vertical nomenclatures, based on genres. It does not mention who can be called an artist: by that time, the identification of the artwork was an adequate clue to recognize its author as an artist. Furthermore, it does not insist on the fixation of an idea as an imperative condition, nor does it mention originality. Copyright protects the expression of ideas: being

83 Ronan Deazley, Martin Kretschmer, Lionel Bently, *Privilege and Property. Essay on the History of Copyright*, Oxford: Open Books Pub., 2010.

84 Barbara Pierre, "Classification of Property and Conceptions of Ownership in Civil and Common Law" 28 *Revue générale de droit* 1997, pp. 235–274.

unconcerned with questions about the creativity, genius or aesthetics of a work, it protects any expression as long as it originates from its creator.

Unable to provide a full harmonization, the Convention calls for the intervention of single national legislations:

> It shall, however, be a matter for legislation in the countries of the Union to prescribe that works in general or any specified categories of works shall not be protected unless they have been fixed in some material form (art. 2.2).

When confronting UCB taxonomies with the challenges of contemporary art, one can notice a couple of major problems:

- its vagueness on some issues, far from providing a standard for the global harmonization of copyright law, leaves this area undefined and to be addressed by national laws: in particular, this is the case of the *originality* requirement;
- the Convention, as amended, does not cope with some artistic manifestations that emerged over the last few decades; while it hints at transformative art, it is silent on hybrid artworks. In fact, its vertical categories are a limit which applies outdated boundaries to artistic expressions explicitly made to trespass the traditional frames of visual art.[85]

The taxonomy adopted by UCB, however, is just as outdated as that found in national legislations. It will be sufficient to recall the classification of genres under British law:

> Copyright law in the United Kingdom has a troubled relationship with the visual arts. Though ostensibly designed to encourage their progress in an even-handed and value-neutral manner, it effectively discriminates between them: it protects the established arts of painting, sculpture, architecture, photography and drawing, for example, but implicitly excludes some contemporary practices in the visual arts completely (e.g. body art, land art, and performance art in general); radically limits the protection available to others (e.g. installation art, conceptual art, minimalist art);

85 Nor are other international instruments, like EU regulations and directives or TRIP agreements, of help in this regard. See Barbara Pasa, "Industrial Design and Artistic Expression. The Challenge of Legal Protection" 4.1 *Art and Law*, New York, Leiden, Boston: Brill, 2020, p. 29.

> and condemns outright those forms which contradict its rules (e.g. appropriation art).[86]

All over the world, law is in trouble when confronted with the kaleidoscope of techniques and procedures aimed at transcending the boundaries between art and research, art and social\political activism, art and pop culture. Things are similar whenever the law has to deal with art actions that can be widely described as "hybrid":[87]

- autonomous sculptures
- performances and stage projects
- media architectures
- media based interventions in public spaces
- mechatronics \ kinetics \ robotics
- location based and geospatial storytelling
- annotation software tools
- artificial life
- transgenic art
- software art, generative art.

We can now fully understand the modernity of Kant's synthesis. In a few lines he caught the essence of copyright law: a legal relation among three subjects: author, producer, public. The object, though governed by property law as a transferable item, is also determined in its legal status by the author's personal rights. And where those personal rights were emphasized as part of the personal identity (the case of France) there was a more fragile protection of the public interest in experiencing the artwork.

For a long time, the legal status of the subject\artist was not of too much interest within copyright laws. For centuries, until the Renaissance, visual arts were largely made by unknown authors, who worked on commission, producing a set of requested works. A belief in creativity as the result of collective

86 Anne Barron, "Copyright Law and the Claim of Arts", 4 *Intellectual Property Quarterly*, 2002, p. 384.

"Where an artefact cannot have a permanent existence because of the material with which it is made, it cannot be a sculpture as a matter of law". *J & S Davis (Holdings) Ltd v. Wright Health Group Ltd*, Reports of Patent, Design and Trade Mark Cases, Volume 105, Issue 18, 1988, 403–415, p. 403.

87 "In art forms, hybridity could mean the blurring of traditional distinct boundaries between artistic media such as painting, sculpture, film, performance, architecture, and dance. It also can mean cross-breeding art-making with other disciplines, such as natural and physical science, industry, technology, literature, popular culture, or philosophy. Hybrid art forms expand the possibilities for experimentation and innovation in contemporary art": http://schools.walkerart.org/arttoday/index.wac?id=2355.

endeavors became dominant following Vico's representation of Homer and Dante as those who gave shape "to the rather shapeless material produced by the peoples to which they belonged".[88]

When the first national copyright laws (early 18th century) were adopted, the perception of the artist as the master of the artistic process (Romanticism) had still to come. Therefore, the theoretical framework defining creativity was somehow dependent on the past. Hence, the representation of copyright as a set of rules based on a kind of special property right implied a sort of spontaneous recognition of the "Who" as the maker of any *oeuvre* framed within the classification of artistic genres based on the classical tradition.[89]

Only the appearance of Romanticism revealed the conception of art as the expression of subjective *pathos*, thus linking the recognition of the value in artworks with the intensity of the artist's feeling and the outstanding quality of their imagination. The most powerful intellectual movement of the 19th century, driven by a combination of philosophical and political thinking, changed the perception of artists from implicit to explicit:

> Romanticism shifted the theoretical framework for understanding the question of authorship, binding it to the idea of genius, absolute creativity, and uniqueness. Those properties, which identify the maker-creator, were then transposed on the work, which in turn became a unique object, an irreproducible one of a kind, an object bearing the aura theorized by Walter Benjamin. *In the Romantic understanding of the subject, an artwork has a strong dependence on its maker.*[90] [emphasis added]

While recollecting these steps in the history of modern art, one understands the validity of the statement that "art bears no limits". When authors embraced Romanticism they embraced an attitude aimed to *transcend the limits* and this had an impact on the perception of the object\artwork. The classification of genres which had informed copyright laws was blown to pieces; the mirror reflecting reality broke into a kaleidoscopic and fragmented set of different images.

In other words, the Romantic acclamation of the artist as a demiurge nested the rupture of the aesthetic canon performed by Duchamp with his "readymade". Innumerable waves of new artistic movements expanded that rupture. Not only the styles and the subjects were new: the traditional hierarchies

88 Tiziana Andina, "What is Art?" quoted fn. 76, p. 60.

89 Anne Barron, quoted fn. 85, p. 384.

90 Tiziana Andina, "What is Art?", quoted *supra* fn. 76, p. 61.

contained within the concept of "artistic genre" were also challenged and overturned by a search of new media and the rejection of the past.[91] "Fighting the Academies", thus, also meant struggling against consolidated styles and modes, the ones which for centuries had governed the grouping of similar artworks.

Traditional theories in aesthetics had shared with copyright laws the assumption that all arts could be confined within a closed list of mutually exclusive expressive genres, each with an essential character, and that norms for each of those arts (whether aesthetic or proprietary norms) could derive from the self-contained technical conditions and demands of their production.

At this crossroads of art history, the art world and the world of law went separate ways: the breaking of the canon paved the way to an era of awkwardness within the legal discourse as to the identification of the "Who" and the "What" of art. Deprived of the reassuring map designed by the traditional genres in visual arts, judges entered a "*terra incognita*": the identification of "what" art is.

The "ready-made" experiments made it clear that art can be defined through a process of stipulation; the same that would be best defined, later on, by John Searle with his formula "*X counts as Y in C*".[92] There is no need to prove that today, according to Searle, the art world is a "*C*"; therefore, we may use his formula in two different variations:

1) a work counts as art as long as it is so defined by the art world, or
2) an author is an artist as long as they are so defined by the art world.

This frame was developed outside of the world of the law. There is much evidence of this; one may refer to the rich set of judicial cases displaying how judges are not at ease when called to solve ontological queries posed by contemporary art. Slowly, however, a new judicial reasoning has arisen: one that

---

91 "An artistic *genre*, so understood, is not a mere cluster of features that allows us to classify works of art. Rather, an artistic *genre* is the outcome of a historical process that constitutes the genre as a practice centered on a medium. As a practice, a genre such as literature has its own history as well as an institution such a university has its own history [...]. An artistic *genre* can be seen as a historical chain in which the works of art belonging to that *genre* have their place". Angela Condello and Enrico Terrone, "Genre Classification: A Problem of Normativity and Exemplarity", in Werner Gephart and Jure Leko (eds.), *Law and the Arts. Elective Affinities and Relationships of Tension*, Frankfurt a./M.: Klostermann, 2017, 39–46, p. 41.

92 John Searle, *The Construction of Social Reality*, New York: Free Press, 1995 as discussed by Tiziana Andina, quoted fn. 76, p. 47ff. A similar approach was adopted by George Dickie: his definition of art involves two characteristics: (1) is the object an artefact, that is, is it made by someone and (2) is it a social property, that is, has it been conferred with "the status of [a] candidate for appreciation by some person or persons acting on behalf of the art world." George Dickie, *Art and Aesthetics. An Institutional Analysis*, NY: Cornell UP, 1974, p. 34.

was based on the identification of the nature of the subject\author and, at a later stage, on the search for a "context".

If it is no longer possible to identify the artist\subject through the consideration of their "beautiful and personally crafted work"; if what remains is a gesture incorporating an idea, how can a judge, called to decide what is and what isn't art, refrain from investigating the *role of the author*? To exist, art needs a normative discourse. Art does exist, however, also without the law, even against it.

Whenever we try to apply regularity (order, predictability) to a succession of facts, we recognize that no stipulation is possible if we do not partake in a set of definitions and mechanisms, which we need to call a phenomenon "significant". This also applies to the art world, where some indexes of validation are held as normative by a community (artists, curators, dealers, collectors, experts) for a certain period of *time*, and within a given *space*. Those indexes may change, evolve, and their transformation is recorded. The art world, in other words, has the privilege to say what is art and what is not.

The world of law has no such privilege; it needs to lean upon the art world to implement its protection. And when what is defined by the art world as "artistic" does not fit the formal requirements of the law, then there is no legal protection. But lack of legal protection does not necessarily mean lack of artistic identity. In fact, artworks did "exist" long before the first elementary copyright regulations were adopted.

Summing up and explaining the kaleidoscope metaphor: the race run throughout the 20th century between visual arts and the law ended up with no winners. Both Art and the Law were placed at the same starting line: at the time the Berne Convention was adopted, artists as subjects of the law and artworks as objects of the law were clearly identifiable. Established genre classifications were able to define the reality of artistic production. The mirror was still unbroken. However, it did not last too long, as many challenges brought by the different avant-gardes to classic law disrupted the canons of beauty, of genre distinction, as well as of permanence of the works in time and space. The world of law had to come to terms with the odd nature of ready-made works, and then with conceptual artists, who had removed materiality from their artistic action.

Let us consider, for example, a work by Giuseppe Pietroniro: *Repositioning furniture*:[93] it consists of redistributing and repositioning furniture in the buyer's home, according to modalities decided by the artist. The project aims to transform the original function of the objects and, consequently, also that

93 https://giuseppepietroniro.com/gmedia-album/roomates/#!.

of the surrounding living space. The purchaser has to pay only for the artist's travelling costs, and to provide him with housing and food in the same room where the artist will be working, for the time needed.

There are thousands of such installations in art practice, but copyright law is not able to offer its protection. Performance art was born, among other things, as a reaction against the commodification of art and the art market. Insofar as copyright is based on property and protects economic rights, it is by design incapable of handling performance art.

Without a pre-existent regulation, the interested parties can enter voluntary agreements to protect their interests and determinations: a solution which has proven to be quite efficient, but that requires a proactive attitude toward the use of contracts and the capacity to avoid the risk of invalidity due to the absence of an "object". A core question, then, remains: what is the minimum grade of material required by the law to give substance to an idea?

From the perspective of copyright law, the problem with these practices is that they do not conform to any of the species accommodated by the legal definition of "artistic work".[94] If they are characterized as art by the art world, this is not because they can be described as paintings or sculptures, but simply because their making is accompanied by the claim that "this is art" and calls for an aesthetic judgement on the part of the viewer.

Anne Barron lucidly said:

> As far as the artist is concerned, two consequences flow from this way of thinking about the objects of copyright. First, it has resulted in their being disaggregated into a series of classifications and subclassifications that appear highly anomalous from the perspective of the contemporary artist, whose practice can no longer be confined by the categories of painting, drawing, sculpture, collage, engraving, architecture or even photography. There is no specific sub-classification of the 'artistic work' category that could accommodate installation art, video art, environmental art, body art, performance art, mixed media works or most conceptual art; nor is there a general overarching category of 'art' that could accommodate the products of these practices.[95]

---

94 Performance Art, e.g., has not been considered in some copyright national regulations as a visual art category, while some countries allow copyright protection for performances, but not for the category of film works.

95 Anne Barron, quoted fn. 85, p. 387.

Today copyright law is struggling; depending on 19th-century categories of property law and art classifications, it has been often bypassed, if not ignored, by artists. The Berne Convention, conceived to protect in an effective and uniform manner the rights of authors in their literary and artistic works, over time proved to be unable to cope with the acceleration and unpredictability of contemporary practices. Worldwide, copyright protection means different things, depending on the jurisdiction and the context; moral rights, the protection of site-specific art, formal requirements of expression, with or without fixation, offer the most instructive examples of diversity among national laws.

Therefore, many art practices remain deprived of protection, particularly within the area of conceptual art, or assisted by alternative remedies, mainly from the realm of contract law. And all this happened far before AI-generated *oeuvres* brought in further irritation to the legal world.

The divide between the legal world and the art world on the ontological demarcation of *what* is art has become irredeemable. Rather than predicating a readjustment of copyright laws (which would recall the Zeno's paradox of Achilles and the tortoise, where Achilles is the law, doomed to run hopelessly after the arts), we should look, as Alessandra Donati explained, at the flexible instruments provided by the law of contracts.[96]

4 Artificial Authors?

"Can a computer be an author?" is an enticing query, because it raises questions on the nature of creativity, autonomy, and human expression. No univocal answer is available. In fact, affirmative voices have been heard within the art world, while legal experts are largely leaning towards the negative.

We have seen artists conceive their artworks without physical touch, as their making is based on instructions given to a crafter. The identification of the author as the sole creator of an artistic idea *and* executor of the work has become an obsolete representation. Still, copyright laws keep maintaining that, to be relevant for protection, a work must be *authored*, and *original*.[97] How, then,

96 See Alessandra Donati, quoted fn. 8, pp. 126–157.

97 The Berne Convention mentions a *fixation* requirement, though in nonbinding terms: "It shall be a matter for legislation in the countries of the Union to prescribe that works in general or any specified categories of works shall not be protected unless they have been fixed in some material form" (Art. 2.2.). This phrasing is meant to allow the Convention's member countries to determine autonomously whether they wish to impose a requirement that the work seeking protection be fixed in a tangible format, that it need not be fixed at all, or that it must meet some other standard in between these extremes.

does AI-generated art place itself in the frame of the evolving notion of authorship in contemporary art?

There is good evidence that, a century after Duchamp, and regardless of many contemporary artists' work to disband the stereotype of the artist as a lonely and unpredictable genius,[98] we still stand in the shadow of late romanticism, when it was conventional to pay great attention to the solitary author's sentiment. According to Peter Jaszi:

> the picture of solitary authors creating original ideas *ex nihilo* through their intellectual labors lies at the *normative heart* of our vision of copyright.[99]

According to most countries' legislation, non-human copyright is not acceptable.[100] Norms and regulations belonging to different legal orders insist on "human nature" as the prime mover of creativity. This paradigm is firmly rooted in classic copyright law and has resisted criticisms over the years, from that given by the French postmodernist school of thought (Michel Foucault,[101] Roland Barthes[102]) to that raised, more recently, by scholars like Martha Woodmansee or Mark Rose, who have maintained that

---

See Megan Carpenter and Steven Hetcher, "Function over Form: Bringing the Fixation Requirement into the Modern Era", 82 *Fordham L. Rev.* 2014, 2221–2271.

98 The artists that already in the late 1950s and early 1960s were active in questioning the role of the artist as a solitary genius include the Swiss sculptor Jean Tinguely. His machines were designed to produce art works. With a series of works named *Métamatics*, Tinguely not only problematized the introduction of the robotic machine as an interface in our society, but also questioned the relationship among artists, artworks and viewers.

99 Peter Jaszi, "Toward a Theory of Copyright: The Metamorphoses of Authorship", *Duke L.J.* 1991, 455–502, p. 500.

100 Following Pamela Samuelson ("Allocating Ownership Rights in Computer Generated Works" 47 *U.Pitt.L.Rev.* 1185, 1985, p. 1199) there is a problem of internal consistency within copyright laws. This was partially originated when U.S. and European legislators passed amendments explicitly recognizing the copyrightability of software, a utilitarian subject matter closer to patent law and unrelated to the tradition of copyright legislations.

101 Michel Foucault, *What Is an Author?*, in Paul Rabinow (ed.), *The Foucault Reader*, 1984 (1969), p. 101 quoted by Caris J. Craig and Ian Kerr, "The Death of the AI Author" *Osgoode Legal Studies Research Paper* 2019, p. 11. Following Craig and Kerr, the establishment of a system of ownership and strict copyright rules (toward the end of the 18th and beginning of the 19th century), for Foucault, was when the author "was accepted into the social order of property which governs our culture." Texts and books *with authors* thus became forms of property and objects of appropriation.

102 Roland Barthes *The Death of the Author*, (Richard Howard, transl., 1967), http://www.ubu.com/aspen/aspen5and6/threeEssays.html#barthes.

> the figure of the romantic author sits monolithically at the core of copyright law, obscuring important realities about the collective nature of creativity and misrepresenting the actual processes of cultural production.[103]

Somewhat paradoxically, one could assume that postmodern theories on the "death of the author" have been nurtured by the perseverance of the idea of the "romantic author": the deeper the perception of the demiurgic role of the Author, the stronger the reaction against it.

A change in the role of the romantic author may affect the position of those receiving the artwork, such as buyers, viewers – in a word, the audience. If the author is no longer the only actor entitled to provide artworks with meaning, this will result in an enhanced appreciation of the context, the creative action and the users' modes of reception. In fact, many artists have explicitly defined the audience as a central component for the completion, recognition and validation of their production.

Questions about a possible definition of an AI-based authorship, therefore, arose in the middle of a stale debate on the "death of the author." Those emerging questions have been then driving critics to find new arguments,[104] while seeking to make copyright law receptive *vis à vis* the most contemporary modes of art making. When authorship is fixed, as it has been, in the human nature of the artist, significant corollaries must be inferred: neither non-human agents, like animals,[105] nor natural events can be recognized as authors.

---

103 Mark Rose, *Authors and Owners. The Invention of Copyright*, Cambridge: Harvard Univ. Press, 1993, p. 3, quoted by Annemary Bridy fn. 11, p. 5. See also Gizela Horvath, "The Rhetoric of Absence in Contemporary Art", Rozália Klára Bakó, Krisztina Bernáth, Éva Bíró Kaszás, Izabella Györgyjakab, Gizella Horváth (eds.) *Argumentor. Proceedings of the Second International Conference on Argumentation and Rhetoric*, Partiumi Kiadó, Oradea and Debrecen University Press, Debrecen, 2012, 175–195.

104 Following, for example, Mark Rose (quoted, fn. 102): "The discourse of original genius and the problems inherent in the reifications of the author and the work persist today, complicating the application of copyright doctrine, and obscur[ing] the fact that cultural production is always a matter of appropriation and transformation" (quoted by Carys Craig and Ian Kerr, "The Death of AI Author", in *Osgoode Legal Studies Research Paper*, May 17, 2019, fn. 35).

105 As legal precedents show, a monkey cannot be the author of a beautiful photograph: the case dates back to 2011, when an Indonesian monkey took a selfie after David Slater, a wildlife photographer, left his camera unattended. Slater published a book containing the monkey's photographs through a self-publishing company (*Blurb Inc.*). An American animal rights organization (People for Ethical Treatment of Animals PETA) tried to use the monkey's selfies to establish a legal precedent that animals should be declared copyright holders. In September 2015 PETA filed a lawsuit against Slater and Blurb, requesting that the monkey be assigned the copyright and that PETA be appointed to

As I said, a reflection on authorship in AI-generated artworks is particularly valuable not only for its capacity to propose new solutions to fill some gaps in the law, but also because it brings scholars and practitioners with different expertise (like software engineers, philosophers, lawyers, curators) to review their positions on the identification of art making as a practice that is less and less made "by hand of the artist".

As has been vividly put by Galanter:

> in modernity the focus of attention is on the author who, at the highest levels of achievement, engages in a high-stakes battle to create a totalizing theory and masterwork. Those working in highly specialized incremental scientific research also don't consider the reader to have a role in authorship per se. The readers are merely the fortunate beneficiaries of the results. And when modernity reigned supreme over the arts, artists were similarly viewed as being singular, potentially heroic, and relatively unconcerned with their audience. From such a view creativity is seen as being solely the domain of the author.[106]

Drawing a line with both modernist and postmodernist perspectives, Galanter wishes for a new approach, a kind of Hegelian synthesis which he names "complexity-based account of creativity":[107]

> [It] has to not only consider the brain function of the author, but also the social context of the creative activity, and the "inputs" to the author prior to a given creation. Of special interest is the nonlinear amplification and modification of creative ideas by readers who go on to contribute to feedback loops.[108]

In my view, the romantic mode of the author as an independent, isolated agent, gifted with the genius of creativity is not only culturally obsolete, but

administer proceeds from the photos for the endangered species' benefit. In dismissing PETA's case, the court ruled that a monkey cannot own copyright under U.S. law. See Andres Guadamuz, "The Monkey Selfie: Copyright Lessons for Originality in Photographs and Internet Jurisdiction", *Internet Policy Review*, 2016, p. 5.

106 Quoted *supra*, fn. 7.

107 "Complex adaptive systems are those complex systems that both sense the changing nature of their surroundings and take actions to maintain their integrity. To the extent a computer can be considered a complex adaptive system it can also be considered creative". Ibid.

108 Ibid.

also overemphasized by the requirements of copyright law. This situation clashes against the challenge brought by AI, due to the irredeemable lack of humanness and consciousness of Artificially Intelligent Machines (AIM).

As a matter of fact, the number of those advocating a reform in copyright law, in order to recognize authorship in AIM, is modest. Many more, at least within the field of legal studies, are those proposing a transformation of authorship by enhancing protection of public interest, also through collaborative copyright and open access.

> If we collectively value and seek to encourage the act of authorship through law and policy, surely it is not the originating, controlling and ultimately mythic romantic authorship that we mean to instigate and reward; rather, the entire point of the social practice of authorship seeks to encourage precisely this discursive participation in the dialogic process of human interaction and the mutually constitutive creation and exchange of text, meaning, and identity.[109]

Promoting an account of authorship that is *relational*, envisaging authorship as a dialogic and communicative artistic act that is inherently social and participated, however, does not necessarily include the so-called "AI author". Cooperation on part of the audience and collaborative authorship remain dependent on a top-down paradigm. This is somehow due to the matrix of copyright law, which presupposes an author.

As is known, the 1886 Berne Convention[110] failed to define authorship; this silence was due to a general understanding that the "true meaning" of the term "author" implied its being human in nature and related to the persons who create copyrightable works.[111]

In the United States, the Federal Copyright Office declared that it will "register an original work of authorship, provided that the work was created by a human being." This statement originates from case law: in Feist Publications vs. Rural Telephone Service Company Inc.,[112] the court ruled that copyright law only protects "the fruits of intellectual labor" that "are founded in the creative powers of the mind."

---

109 Caris Craig and Ian Kerry, quoted fn. 101, p. 16.

110 The Convention is based on three main principles: *national treatment* (works are given the same protection in each country as the country grants to the works of their nationals); *automatic protection* (no formalities required); *independence of protection* (works receive protection even if they cannot obtain such protection in their country of origin).

111 Jane Ginsburg, quoted fn. 37, p. 131.

112 499 U.S. 340 (1991).

More recently, however, the U.S. Copyright Office launched a public review of its internal procedures, proposing a rephrasing apt "to consider the challenge of ascertaining authorship in an era of technology-aided creation". So, a revised draft edition of the very relevant *Compendium of U.S. Copyright Office Practices* was explicitly devoted to *Works That Lack Human Authorship* (Section 303.2):

> As discussed in Section 306, the Copyright Act protects 'original works of authorship.' To qualify as a work of 'authorship' a work must be created by a human being. Works that do not satisfy this requirement are not copyrightable.[113]

Within the European Union, the Court of Justice has ruled several times that copyright only applies to *original* works, and that originality must reflect the "author's own intellectual creation." It is thus usually understood that an original work must reflect the author's personality, meaning that a human author is necessary for a copyrightable work to exist.[114] Likewise, in the EU Member States national laws imply, more or less explicitly, that the "human factor" is the necessary prerequisite to provide copyright protection to authors.

---

113 More precisely: "The U.S. Copyright Office will not register works produced by nature, animals, or plants. Likewise, the Office cannot register a work purportedly created by divine or supernatural beings, although the Office may register a work where the application or the deposit copy(ies) state that the work was inspired by a divine spirit.
Examples:
- A photograph taken by a monkey.
- A mural painted by an elephant.
- A claim based on the appearance of actual animal skin.
- A claim based on driftwood that has been shaped and smoothed by the ocean.
- A claim based on cut marks, defects, and other qualities found in natural stone.
- An application for a song naming the Holy Spirit as the author of the work".

Similarly, the Office will not register works produced by a machine or by a mere mechanical process that operates randomly or automatically without any creative input or intervention from a human author. The crucial question is "whether the 'work' is basically one of human authorship, with the computer [or other device] merely being an assisting instrument, or whether the traditional elements of authorship in the work (literary, artistic, or musical expression or elements of selection, arrangement, etc.) were actually conceived and executed not by man but by a machine". As evident, this rule leaves without protection all works produced without human intervention.

114 ECJ *Infopaq* decision of July 16, 2009 (C-5/08 Infopaq International A/S vs. Danske Dagblades Forening). Also, Council Directive 91/250/EEC, 2009/24/EC, *On the Legal Protection of Computer Programs*: "Authorship of computer programs – The author of a computer program shall be the natural person or group of natural persons who has created the program or, where the legislation of the Member State permits, the legal person designated as the rightholder by that legislation".

UK law deserves a special note, as its copyright legislation contains specific provisions dealing with computer-generated works. According to art. 178 of the UK Copyright Designs and Patent Act (CDPA, 1988), a computer-generated work is defined as "a work that is generated by a computer such that there is no human author". Under art. 9.3 of the same CDPA, authorship of such work is *given to the person by whom the arrangements necessary for the creation of the work are undertaken*. In fact, this is nothing but a legal fiction, set to solve the dilemma of ascertaining authorship in such works, based on the supposition that the computer is nothing more than a tool.[115] Clearly, "the person responsible for making such arrangements is not the true author under copyright law, as evidenced by art. 9.1 CDPA".[116]

According to Colin Davies, then

> in the case of computer-generated works produced by an AI system independently of any further contribution from the original programmer [...] we will find ourselves with either a patent lacking an owner or a copyright work which is orphaned.[117]

To identify as author the person who – following the CDPA wording – "undertakes the necessary arrangements" is not an easy task; thus, the prerogatives of the supposed author could be disputed, should property right entitlement be contested.

---

115 As an exception to the standard duration of copyright (70 years from the end of the calendar year in which the author dies), art. 12.7 states that "If the work is computer-generated the above provisions do not apply and copyright expires at the end of the period of 50 years from the end of the calendar year in which the work was made".

Jani McCutcheon holds that "the link between authorship and conditions for protection is rekindled, as the originality requirement will have to be self-standing and independent of authorship – not linked to the person responsible for the arrangements (as s/he is the author only due to the legal fiction and has no direct connection to the work), but also not linked to the computer", see "Curing the authorless void: protecting computer generated works following Ice TV and Phone Directories", 37 *Melbourne University Law Review* 2013, p. 46.

116 Robert C. Denicola, "Ex Machina: Copyright Protection for Computer-Generated Works", 69 *Rutgers U. L.R.* 251 2016 for a survey of national copyright laws in Ireland, New Zealand, South Africa, Hong Kong and India, emulating the *UK Copyright, Designs and Patents Act* (1988).

117 Colin R. Davies, quoted fn. 25, p. 619. Colin Davies and Ryan Abbott have both (autonomously) argued that computers should be considered legal authors/inventors under relevant Intellectual Property laws. See Ryan Abbott, "I Think, Therefore I Invent: Creative Computers and the Future of Patent Law", 57 *Brit. Col. L. Rev.* 2016, p. 1079ff.

In fact, the scale of AI-systems autonomy is inversely proportional to the implementation of the regime chosen by the CDPA. The more independent from human interference the AI is, the less probable the application of that rule will be, due to the lack of human intervention. British and analogous regulations adopted by some common law jurisdictions on computer-generated works do not seem to be a workable solution to authorial issues in AI-generated works. Even where it would prove to be viable for the case of non-autonomous AI systems, it remains unclear who the "person responsible for the arrangements" is.[118]

Here the split between classical copyright law and the actual state of technology[119] truly stands out. There is no doubt as to whether authorial rights

---

118 Annemarie Bridy has worked out a variation on the theme of "the person undertaking the necessary arrangements": the "work for hire doctrine", codified under art. 101 of the U.S. Copyright Law. The doctrine *provides* that "the employer or *other person for whom the work was prepared* is considered the author". Since AI-generated work would not fall under the traditional definition of work-for-hire, Bridy suggests that the statutory definition could be amended to *incorporate the definition* of computer-generated work from other jurisdictions such as, for example, art. 9.3 of the British CDPA. See Annemarie Bridy, "Coding Creativity" quoted fn. 11. Shlomit Yanisky-Ravid has proposed that AI should be treated as a worker by the person who commissioned the work, following the exception to the general rule established by the U.S. Copyright Law (arts. 101 and 201). The proposal, limited to U.S. law, would require a lawmaker's intervention as, according to the existing law, the hiring party is considered to have control on the manner and means by which the product is accomplished. As seen, this is not the case for independently generated AI work. See Shlomit Yanisky-Ravid quoted fn. 15, p. 659.

The "work for hire doctrine" does not fit AIsystems, as they remain external to the traditional employer-employee relationship as designed by U.S. copyright law. Other proposals to provide legal protection to AI-generated artworks through normative adjustments include the drafting of a regulation similar to the protection of producers or broadcasters, whose protection has a commercial or technical nature. This could be achieved e.g. by recognizing, within civil law countries, neighboring rights, or by expanding the regime of initial ownership of subject-matter other than works (as in Australian law).

See also Massimo Maggiore, "Artificial Intelligence, computer generated works and copyright" in Enrico Bonadio and Nicola Lucchi (eds.), *Non-Conventional Copyright* London: Elgar 2018, 382–400.

119 "It is both possible and necessary to have a copyright law that combines safeguards for free expression, guarantees of due process, mechanisms for access, and respect for intellectual property. To this end, I would like to state something that I hope is uncontroversial: the issues of authors are intertwined with the interests of the public. As the first beneficiaries of the copyright law, they are not a counterweight to the public interest but instead are at the very center of the equation": Maria Pallante (Head of the United States Copyright Office) on March 20, 2013 to the Subcommittee on Courts, Intellectual Property and the Internet Committee on the Judiciary, calling for the U.S. Copyright Law to be updated. Ms. Pallante has submitted that the current law, the majority of which was enacted

should be held by the owner of the software (for example *Word* by Microsoft) or by the actual writer of a poem written using Microsoft Word. However, whenever it is assumed that an AI process based on algorithms created – with no human interference – an "original" and readable poem, the matter turns out to be far from obvious.

The problem, in fact, becomes awkward when the automatically generated output (let's say, a poem or a drawing) cannot be traced back to any human action or interference.[120] As cutting-edge developments in AI research keep marching on, we are moving into an age of "digital authorship", in which digital works will be making other works, indistinguishable from works of human authorship.

There are many recent examples of AI-generated works. There is "Jukedeck", an "Artificially-intelligent music composer, bringing artificial intelligence to music composition and production, a trained deep neural network able to understand music composition at a granular level".[121] Or consider a recurrent neural network named "Benjamin", which authored the script of a short film called "Sunspring", presented at the science fiction London festival in 2016.[122]

These elaborations have already appeared in court,[123] and have renewed a longstanding challenge to the process of adjudication: judges find themselves

way back in 1976, is outdated and no longer provides effective protection to authors of copyright works.

120 The problem is globally spread: "[The]concept of authorship has remained steadfastly physically based on single authorship, while productions have steadily become digital and multi-authored", noticed Jani McCutcheon "The vanishing author in computer-generated works: a critical analysis of recent Australian case law". 36 *Melbourne University Law Review* 2013; 915, p. 967.

121 https://thenextweb.com/insider/2019/07/24/tiktoks-parent-company-appears-to-have-acquired-ai-music-startup-jukedeck/ (last visited January 28, 2020).

122 The movie is advertised on the web with Oscar Sharp as Director, Thomas Middleditch, Humphrey Ker, Elisabeth Gray as main actors and Benjamin, a system-on-chip [SOC] computer with graphics processing unit [GPU], running a 'long short term memory' [LSTM] recurrent neural network [RNN] as Writer.

123 In a case decided by an Australian Federal Court Acohs (Pty. Ltd. vs. Ucorp. Pty. Ltd. [2012] FCAFC 16), the judge declared that a work "generated with the intervention of a computer could not be protected by copyright because it was not produced by a human". And *whenever the source code of a software is not written by persons who can be defined as "author" for the purposes of the Copyright Act, the source code may not fall within the Act's protective provisions.*

According to commentators, the Acohs decision is bound to have an impact on businesses that create digital products, such as inventory recording systems, data interpretation software and the like, just as it may affect businesses' interest to protect digital products under the provisions of the Australian *Copyright Act* (1968, as reformed in 2019).

again bound to make decisions not only on the issue: "what is art?", but also on the matching question: "what is an author?".

A computer program developed for machine learning has an integrated algorithm that allows it to learn from data inputs, so that it can evolve and make future decisions that may be either guided or independent. When applied to art, music and literary works, machine-learning algorithms absorb information from inputs provided by programmers. They "learn" from those inputs (images, texts, any sort of information or measurements) to generate a new work, making independent decisions throughout the process to determine what the new work will look like. An important feature for this type of artificial intelligence is that while programmers can set parameters, the work is actually generated by the computer program itself – referred to as a neural network – in a process which is considered by many to be similar to the thinking process of human beings.

According to existing copyright regulations, an AI independently generated work will not be recognized as an "artwork" in the sense of copyright law and, therefore, will not be subject to the legal protection provided by copyright privileges. In other words, as long as the procedure can be recognized by the law as driven by a human agent and the result of a human mind, the law will be loosely adapted to recognize to the humans, and not to the AI, the guarantees provided by copyright regulations.

When, however, the advancement of technology[124] makes the recognition of the "person making the arrangements for the work" too loose, if not undetectable, there is a legal vacuum. The challenge cannot be faced simply by adjusting copyright laws through minimal amendments. Rather, we should understand that inertia or minimal adjustment will not make up for the uncertainties originated by AI in the copyright systems. This vacuum will generate confusion and judicial irresolution. In fact, the dilemma judges are called to solve flips around these two options:

124 "The Internet revolution of the 1990s caused a harsh crisis with respect to the distribution of artworks and exerted extreme pressure on the existing legal infrastructure for protecting and enforcing copyrights. While this crumbling infrastructure has been propped up by both statutory and technological buttresses designed to curb the unauthorized copying and distribution of digital content, few on either side of the "copyfights" would argue that the system is not broken, and many believe it is irretrievably so": Lawrence Lessig, *Free Culture. How Big Media Uses Technology and the Law to Lock Down Culture and Control Creativity*, New York: Penguin Press, 2004, p. 173 (also Creative Commons).

a) a strict reading of copyright law: if there is no way to provide protection, then the law does not intend to protect AI-generated works; this option would result in leaving AI-generated artworks in the public domain,[125] or

b) assigning the title and the related protections by choosing one or more privileged holders among the different possible ones, such as the *programmer*[126] or the *user*.[127]

Option *a*) enjoys support in the literature;[128] it sounds quite consistent with the increasing favor gained by open-source policies. Those who see it as a bad choice stand on the side of those utilitarian theories[129] that have nurtured, at least in the U.S. world, the legal regime of arts.

Option *b*) is more articulated. In particular with regards to the *programmer*: granting authorship and all related privileges to the programmer would mean that they are automatically the owner of everything the program is able to generate. This solution is nothing but over-rewarding for the programmer, if we consider the possibility that they have likely not envisaged the work designed by the creative machine.

According to Pamela Samuelson:

> As strong as these pro-programmer arguments may seem, there are some strong reasons why the computer program author should not be given rights in all works generated by use of his program [...]. By keeping the program to himself and copyrighting every piece of music or patenting every nonobvious chemical formula that the program generates, the programmer would be able to prevent others from obtaining interests in the program's output. If he does this, of course, the programmer will not

125 See Ana Ramalho, "*Will robots rule the (artistic) world? A proposed model for the legal status of creations by artificial intelligence systems*", 2017. https://papers.ssrn.com/sol3/papers.cfm?abstract_id=2987757.

126 A *programmer* (also called *coder*) is an individual who writes computer software or applications by giving the computer specific programming instructions.

127 *Users* are the people (or other systems) for whom the software is written.

128 See Ralph D. Clifford, "Intellectual Property in the Era of the Creative Computer Program: Will the True Creator Please Stand Up?", 71 *Tul. L. Rev.* 1997, p. 1675. He claims that output generated by creative computers cannot and should not be protected by intellectual property laws and that such results should be in the public domain. Perraya and Margonia also propose the solution of the public domain; see Aaron Perraya and Thomas Margoni, "From music tracks to Google Maps: Who owns computer generated works?" 26 *Comp. L. and Sec. Rev.* 2010, p. 621.

129 See Annemarie Bridy, "Fearless Girl Meets Charging Bull: Copyright and the Regulation of Intertextuality", 9 *UC Irvine Law Review*, 2019, p. 293. She describes the clash between the "Continental view of copyright as a guarantor of authorial supremacy and the more utilitarian, public orientation of the U.S. copyright law".

> make any money directly from the program, although he may profit from selling the output that the program generates. Thus, the programmer has a choice, and should not complain about the consequences of his choice to market the program.[130]

There are also problems with regard to the *user*: the person who seems to be directly concerned by the computer-generated work and able to give it a perceptible form. However, one should not read this situation and refer to "classical copyright law", where the author is the one who gives expression to the idea. Quite the opposite, what is produced by a creative machine is more than a pure idea, and what is operated by a user can be less than the action of giving expression. In fact, it would make little sense to consider the user as the author "by default" whenever the entitlement cannot be given to the programmer. In fact, a user might have no control over the final AI-made work.

As one may suppose, even within the scope of AI-generated artworks, the process is less linear than expected. There are, moreover, cases when the generator program, instead of producing final outputs, produces unfinished works: who is to be considered the "author" in these cases? Or, following a similar line of reasoning, could not we apply the "derivative work" scheme[131] to AI-generated works, in order to split entitlements? And what about the case of a user intervening on the final product independently created by the system? Shall we consider the work at their free disposal, as the first founder of an orphan work?

The complexity of these situations puts them all into a grey zone of (un)regulated entitlement, because classic law requires:

- authorship rights to be conferred to humans, and
- that human authors generate not only an idea but also a mode of expression that connects the idea to them.

As to the *derivative work* option, in theory one could argue that the generated output is a *derivative result* of the primary copyrighted program; this would extend copyright protection to anyone holding a copyright in the algorithm. A quite convincing counterargument, however, is that whenever an AI system

---

130 Quoted *supra* fn. 99, p. 1200.
One should also consider that, within EU law, the programmer will not be left without legal defense. The Software Directive 2009/24/EC establishes protection of computer programs, entailing that the programmer can claim rights to the AIsoftware itself.

131 A derivative work is a work based upon one or more pre-existing works, such as a translation, musical arrangement, dramatization, fictionalization, motion picture version, sound recording, art reproduction, abridgment, condensation, or any other form in which a work may be recast, transformed, or adapted.

produces an output independently, the scheme could not apply, simply because machine-generated works, being "the first work", lack the requirements to be qualified as derivative. Let's consider human art: a first work is not (according to the law) derivative from the artist as, although the work depends on the activity of the artist, they are ontologically and formally distinct. Likewise, in AI-made art there is an asymmetry between the formal properties or the ontological nature of the outcome (an artefact) and whatever came before.

The "human factor", then, remains at the center of the stage. Its permanence, however, has not prevented a flourishing of proposals aiming to find a way out of the maze of incomplete legal regulations and outdated normative theories, to adjust copyright laws to the progressing state of technology. The most challenging of these proposals are the ones addressed to consider "AI-driven non-human agents" as potential subjects of law, also looking at new theories developed within the field of law of robots.[132]

> "A corporate body has under UK law legal recognition as an individual" – contends Colin Davies – "a computer which is more akin to a true person, more particularly with the new generation of artificial intelligent computers, should be accorded the same status. This will enable us to attribute authorship of computer-generated works/inventions to the body best entitled to them, the computer, and allow the respective claims of interested parties to be determined not by arbitrary rules of law, but by the parties themselves, through negotiated contractual terms. Revolutionary this may be, but no more so than granting intellectual property rights, as we currently do, to a body corporate".[133]

A brief comparative survey of legal systems may reduce the taxonomy of legal personalities[134] to two main groups: human beings and legal entities (like corporations, foundations, etc.). A more accurate assessment, however, would expand the classification to other agents, like: normal human beings;

132 See Ugo Pagallo, *The Law of Robots. Crime, Contracts and Torts*, Dordrecht: Springer 2013 pp. 155–181. See also Lawrence Solum, "Legal Personhood for Artificial Intelligences", 70 *North Carolina L. Rev.* 1992, 1231–1287, who discusses the three arguments usually brought against the recognition of personhood to AI: 1. "AI systems are not human"; 2. "The Missing-Something Argument"; 3. "AI systems ought to be property".

133 Colin R. Davies quoted fn. 24, p. 618.

134 Worldwide, the concept of "legal person" refers to the ability to participate in the fundamental relationships regulated by the law – such as the capability to own property, enter a contract, file a lawsuit, be named in a lawsuit, serve as a legal principal, and serve as a legal agent.

other human beings (infants); supernatural beings (like angels, spirits); animals; inanimate objects (like idols); associations and incorporated entities (corporations).[135] This classification sounds odd only if we consider contemporary "Western Law" as the only acceptable paradigm. Not only did ancient legal systems include angels and other supernatural entities within the number of persons vested with legal personality, but even today we count legal systems where idols receive some forms of personhood from the law.[136]

Scholarly proposals to recognize *de iure condendo* some elements of legal personhood to AI-driven robots are spreading out, and those advocating this option

> have not only asserted that none of the arguments against the full-fledged personality of such machines are consistent but have even questioned the anthropocentric basis of today's legal framework.[137]

If not redundant, the literature on the matter of authorship and AI-generated art has become abundant.[138] Beside those denying the relevance of the issue we count now a group of commentators who articulate their position on the grounds of utilitarian theories.[139]

It is not only copyright law, then, which is confronted by the emergence of AI-generated art. Constitutional law and private law, two main containers of regulation on legal personality, capacity and status, are also challenged by the emergence of academic theories advocating a legal standing for AI-driven robots. The debate is multidisciplinary, as it impinges on philosophy (the free will argument), psychology (self-consciousness issues), ethics (moral accountability) and, of course, law.

As Samir Chopra and Laurence White contend:

> the conditions for each kind of legal personality could, in principle, be met by artificial agents in the right circumstances. We suggest that objections

135 Sheikh Solaiman, "Legal personality of robots, corporations, idols and chimpanzees: a quest for legitimacy", 25 *Artif. Intell. Law* 2017, 155–179.

136 On the discussion *re* recognition of legal personality to animals see https://www.nonhumanrights.org/litigation-2/.

137 Ugo Pagallo, quoted *supra* fn. 132, p. 159.

138 A survey in Carys Craig and Ian Kerr, quoted fn. 100.

139 See Mihaly Csikszentmihalyi, *Engineering Creativity in an Age of Artificial Intelligence*, Springer, Dordrecht, 2018; James Grimmelman, "Copyright for Literate Robots" 101 *Iowa L. Rev.* 2016, 657–681.

> to such a status for them are based on a combination of *human chauvinism* and a misunderstanding of the notion of legal person.[140]

Returning to authorship and AI: we cannot, I believe, use an analogical argument and say that because of a kind of "human chauvinism" we remain caught within the borders of human authorship as a necessary standard for regulation. AI artefacts are, by their nature, not comparable to human artefacts; they may look similar, even more "beautiful", but they are not the result of, among other things. human emotions. An AI artwork made without direct human co-operation is an output that lacks "the self-expression of its maker".[141]

So far I have looked at the law. Its letter says that whenever there is no human author, there is no copyright protection. Therefore, whenever new generation AI-machines autonomously produce *oeuvres* without human input, those works are in the public domain. Lacking a clear identification of an author, copyright law leaves the works out of its consideration.

Let us now shift the attention from the *subject* to the *object*: non-human intelligent agents, not qualified by the law as "authors", can independently produce works that are remarkable for their aesthetic impact. Whether those works can be qualified as "artworks" depends, sometimes, on the law, but more particularly on the *art world*.[142]

In fact, an artwork is not only what is defined by the law:[143] as art historians have repeatedly proven, the art world is able to recognize works that escape any legal classification. Here's an example: *All We'd Ever Need is One Another* is a mixed-media installation apt to autonomously create images via self-generating scanning techniques. It is defined as a "continuously running art-factory operating independently of human input".[144] The installation generates images using two flatbed scanners, with scanning surfaces pointing at one another. A computer script creates spontaneous mouse movements, randomizing the settings of the proprietary scanning software interface, and launching a scanning process.

Each image is then analyzed by a set of deep-learning algorithms trained on a database of contemporary artworks. When an image matches an

140 Samir Chopra, Laurence White, *A Legal Theory for Autonomous Artificial Agents*, Ann Arbor, Univ. Of Michigan Press, 2011, p. 27, quoted by Ugo Pagallo (above, fn. 131), p. 160.

141 See Deniz Kurt, *Artistic Creativity in Artificial Intelligence*, Nijmegen: Radboud Univ. 2018.

142 On Arthur Danto and the art world see Tiziana Andina, quoted fn. 76, p. 38.

143 Leonard D. Duboff, "Toward a Legal Definition of Art", 12 *Hastings Communications & Entertainment L.J.* 1990, p. 303.

144 http://allwedeverneed.com/about.html.

existing artwork beyond an 83% match, it uploads it to a website and a twitter account.[145]

> These images I describe are created by two desktop scanners directed at each other, reading the way light hits the glass on their counterpart, the way light emanates from one to the other. The two scanners are fixed one in front of the other, but movement is built into them and reflected on them. They mirror the light conditions in the room where they are set: when you see an abstract pictogram, you could be looking at the moon. Or at the strip of light in one of the scanners. They make landscapes that meld the site and the tool.[146]

On a different note, it is hard not to recall the "generative art movement,"[147] dedicated to the exploration of "computational creativity" through a set of practices whereby the artist "cedes control to a system" that is "self-contained enough to operate autonomously".[148]

When we question the art world as embodied by curators, experts, philosophy of arts scholars, and dealers, we find that what makes something an *artwork* is not necessarily based on the identification of a possible human author. The art world deploys a wider set of arguments than the legal world and has greater capacity to transform a theory into an experience through a performative statement.

Better connections between the two worlds could be reached by encouraging multidisciplinary approaches to the notion of authorship. In this sense, grounding his proposal on the "Actor-Network" theory developed by Bruno Latour,[149] Deniz Kurt has recommended an original, and quite radical, attitude towards AI as an art-maker:

---

145 Ibid.

146 Orit Gat, excerpt from Exhibition Primer: http://allwedeverneed.com/about.html.

147 *See* Margaret Boden and Ernest A. Edmonds, "What is Generative Art?", 20 *Digital Creativity* 2009, 21–46, p. 24 explaining that "both in music and in visual arts, the use of the term defines works produced by the activation of a set of rules *and* where the artist lets a computer system take over at least some of the decision-making".

148 See Philip Galanter, "Thoughts on Computational Creativity", 2009 www.semanticscholar.org/paper/30566694e9da20909dafaac77a5d3a022c7b6efa.

149 Graham Harman, *Prince of Networks: Bruno Latour and Metaphysics*, Melbourne: re.Press, 2009. "As a sociological methodology which is based on the philosophy of science, Bruno Latour's Actor-Network Theory (ANT) does not only deal with humans as agents in society. It also focuses on the relations between an actor and the network around it. The 'actor' is not necessarily a human subject, it refers to anything with the ability to act or produce action. Inanimate objects that we use in our everyday life can also be actors because they do

> I would like to suggest that the attribution of 'art' as an approval or evaluation of an output is ultimately defined by the audience. For example, when someone creates a painting, can he or she decide whether it is a piece of art or not? Even if the art-maker claims that it is art for him/her due to his/her intentions of expressing an aesthetical and emotional phenomenon, ultimately the quality of artwork depends on the perception of the audience. [...] Art is a way of communicating embedded in human culture. Therefore, even though the art-maker is a computational program which does not have any intentions to express a certain feeling, the artworks can create an emotional or aesthetical feedback by the human audience.[150]

As mentioned, one may find the point made by Kurt quite (if not too) radical. However, AI undeniably pushes to the forefront a way of understanding art where the social network[151] related to the artistic practice does not involve an author in the traditional, human sense. The outputs of AI may very well be of a quality such that they can sustain enjoyable appreciation in ways that are not dissimilar from those found in more traditional art genres. This happens in spite of the fact that copyright laws struggle to deal with it.

The structure of traditional copyright law, being modelled on property law, is not designed to trace situations where authors, artworks and users tend to melt; this has already been proven by contemporary visual arts, which brought quite a number of challenges to copyright law. Also, copyright law is almost silent on the relationship between the artist and the work.[152]

The new friction brought by AI in visual arts mirrors a previous case of friction between art and law – one that was due to conceptual art. The innovation brought by the latter was focused on the *object*: it dematerialized the *opus*, leaving the work unfinished, pursuing the involvement of the public, selling an abstract "right to perform". In so doing, conceptual artists, with their very different techniques and processes, took art beyond the object, searching

---

things themselves and 'enable us to do things'. Therefore, as Latour argued, both humans and technological artifacts can be actors [...]. According to ANT, an actant can literally be anything, as long as it is granted to be the source of any action. Therefore, ANT approach provides a methodology to be freed from the restrictions of anthropocentrism in art", Deniz Kurt, quoted fn. 141, p. 64.

150 Deniz Kurt, p. 52.

151 See Dominic McIver Lopes, "Beauty: the Social Network", 47 *Canadian J. Phil.* 2017, 437–453. See also Dominic McIver Lopes, *A Philosophy of Computer Art*, Routledge: London, New York, 2009.

152 In fact, even the protection of site-specific art is focused on the reputation of the artist, rather than on the artist-artwork bond.

elsewhere – in the certificate, in the deed – evidence to prove the existence of their artistic idea.[153] And while conceptual art was irritating to the law due to the *problematic identification of a non-object as an artwork*, in the case of AI-generated artworks the disconcert is due to the *problematic identification of a non-author*.

Some scholars[154] have stressed the role of the audience in receiving an AI-generated artwork. While introducing the concept of AI as an agent, autonomously endowed with a goal, Kurt overturns the conventional top\down (author\audience) situation with a "bottom-up perspective, from the human perceiver to the art object".[155] Now, is this suggestion helpful to solve the *impasse* experienced by copyright law as to AI art production?

As said, a conservative configuration of authorship still informs copyright laws, and reconciling existing law with the practice of AI-generated artworks seems to be beyond any reasonable hermeneutical effort. A "bottom-up perspective" could bring useful arguments for the recognition of AI-generated *oeuvres* as art, not for the search of a legal qualification for authorship.

Different views for an innovative legal analysis of the relationship between human and non-human agents stem from a discussion, emerging from the literature, on the possible identification of AI-operated machines as "owners" of generated works. This option entails that an artificial intelligent agent acquires legal personhood but does not imply a recognition of authorship. This has been vividly sustained, among others by Gabriel Hallevy, who advocated the recognition of legal personality for AI-operated machines. His point is centered on an analogy between robots and corporations with respect to criminal liability:

> Why should AI entities be different from corporations? AI entities are taking larger and larger parts in human activities, as do corporations. Offenses have already been committed by AI entities or through them. AI entities have no soul, and some AI entities have neither body nor soul. Thus, there is no substantive legal difference between the idea of criminal responsibility imposed on corporations and on AI entities. It would be outrageous not to subordinate them to human laws, as corporations have been. What else is needed?[156]

153 On the alternative measures taken by conceptual artists to provide legal support to their creations, like contracts, documents, certificates, see the seminal work by Alessandra Donati, quoted fn. 5, p. 126ff.

154 See, e.g., Deniz Kurt quoted fn. 141, p. 76.

155 Ibid.

156 Gabriel Hallevy, "Unmanned vehicles. Subordination to criminal law under the modern concept of criminal liability" 21 *J. Law, Information & Soc.* 2011, p. 211.

More literature has recently been published about the idea that autonomy, creativity, and advancement of AI systems should lead to their recognition as independent subjects vested with limited patrimonial rights and duties:[157]

> the corporation as a legal entity can serve as a basis for imposing rights and duties on AI systems. Corporations are legal entities subject to a legal regime, including corporate, labor, and even criminal law. Therefore, the question relating to AI entities has become 'does the growing intelligence of AI entities subject them, as any other legal entity, to legal social control?'[158]

The proposal of a legal status for intelligent machines, although discussed both at the *political*[159] and at the *legal* level, remained, so far, confined within

---

157 Samir Chopra, Laurence F. White, *A Legal Theory for Autonomous Artificial Agents* Mich. Univ. Press, 2011, 1–3 (arguing for the legal personhood of an artificial agent that will soon be independent and discussing the artificial agent as capable of having "knowledge" and decision-making abilities).

158 Shlomit Yanisky-Ravid, quoted fn. 15, p. 670. There are several consequences to this approach. In Europe, for example, there is a movement arguing that robots should pay taxes. If measured through the lens of copyright law, this approach could result in the AI systems' ownership of the intellectual property of products and processes. See Abbott, quoted *supra* note 109, p. 1080 (arguing that computers are already generating patentable subject matters qualifying as inventors and overtaking human inventors as the primary source of new discoveries and inventions and therefore, that AI should receive patent rights in their inventions). See also John Frank Weaver, *Robots are people too: how Siri, Google Car and Artificial Intelligence Will Force Us to Change our Laws*, Santa Barbara: Praeger 2014, 3–4.

159 Reference must be made to a political declaration adopted by the EU and named: *Copyright for Creativity – A Declaration for Europe*. Issued on 5 May 2010, it was intended as a statement on how *copyright policy* could be constructed in the Internet Age. It comes against the background of political debate in Europe to rethink *copyright* in an era where the use of digital content without paying fees to the creators is part of the business model for some of the largest global internet platforms. The interests of content creators and online platform providers collide.

The declaration was written by a group from the political party "*European People's Party*" (EPP):

"*The development of new technologies underpinning the* ***knowledge economy*** *calls for a review of the copyright acquisition. Together, we need to create greater incentives to maximise creativity, innovation, education and access to culture, and secure Europe's competitiveness.*

Exclusive rights stimulate investment and the production of cultural and knowledge-based goods. Simultaneously, exceptions to those rights create a balanced system that allows for the use of creative works to support innovation, creation, competition and the public interest. Well-crafted exceptions can serve both goals: preserving rewards and incentives for creators while also encouraging innovative re-uses that benefit the public.*

a narrow circle of proponents. The main counterargument is well known: the law acknowledges personality for corporations in all legal systems, but corporations are constituted by human beings. Rights and duties accompanying the

---

While exclusive rights have been adapted and harmonized to meet the challenges of the knowledge economy, copyright's exceptions are radically out of line with the needs of the modern information society. The lack of harmonization of exceptions hinders the circulation of knowledge-based goods and services across Europe. The lack of flexibility within the current European exceptions regime also prevents us from adapting to a constantly changing technological environment.

Europe requires a balanced, flexible and harmonized system of exceptions that is in step with the 21st Century knowledge economy. The European Commission took a first step with the publication of the Green Paper, "Copyright in the Knowledge Economy." The signatories of this declaration call upon the European Commission, the European Parliament and Member States to take this Declaration into account and engage in policy and norm-setting on copyright exceptions to:

Harmonise Exceptions Across Europe: Copyright regulates the flow of consumer as well as knowledge goods in the single market. For European citizens and industry alike, the harmonization of exceptions is a necessary step to facilitate cross-border trade and create equality and clarity before the law.

Act as a Spur to Innovation: New technologies make it possible to expand users' access to vast quantities of relevant knowledge and content. Copyright exceptions must support the development and usage of these innovative services, improving European users' access to content.

Support User Creativity and Wider Participation: The Internet has facilitated an unprecedented shift for citizens, from being passive consumers of "broadcast" culture to active creators and participants. Individual users are increasingly involved in content and knowledge creation. The European copyright framework needs to reflect this new interactivity which encourages creativity, cultural diversity and self-expression.

Ensure Accessibility by all Europeans: Exceptions must balance the protection of the creators' rights with the public interest and must fully support access to knowledge and content for people with disabilities – most notably through the use of new technologies.

Support for Education and Research: Information and communication technologies offer new collaborative ways to develop and share educational and research materials. Copyright exceptions that facilitate new technology-based research and education will propel science and learning, and therefore the knowledge economy, exponentially forward.

Facilitate Preservation and Archiving: Digitization of content is offering new opportunities not only to preserve but also extend the accessibility of Europe's knowledge and cultural heritage with wide-reaching and long-term benefits for society as a whole. The copyright framework must support this.

Ensure Monopoly Rights are Regulated in the Online Environment: Limitations and exceptions act to counterbalance the lack of competition that is created by the granting of monopoly rights in copyright law. In order to protect creativity and innovation we must ensure that these monopoly rights are also regulated in the online environment.

Promote these Principles in International Discussions: The principles and objectives we endorse should not apply only to Europeans – they should be at the center of the EU's contributions in any discussions in multilateral and bilateral *fora* it participates in".

legal personality of those entities would therefore always refer to the humans behind the corporate veil: a scheme which seems to be incompatible with the recognition of personhood to AI systems and robots. Those suggestions made reference to industrial robots and self-driving automobiles. Not surprisingly, therefore, they drew the attention of policymakers. As mentioned, the EU Parliament draft Resolution dated 2017[160] recommended that self-learning robots could be granted "electronic personalities":

> Creating a specific legal status for robots in the long run, so that at least the most sophisticated autonomous robots could be established as having the status of electronic persons responsible for making good any damage they may cause, and *possibly applying electronic personality to cases where robots make autonomous decisions or otherwise interact with third parties independently* (par. 59f.) [emphasis added].

Such a status could allow robots to be insured and to be held liable for damages, should they start hurting people or spoiling property. This is an innovative reform shaped within a legal frame comparable to what already exists under the name of "legal personality of corporate entities".[161]

The proposal at first was confined within the text of the draft Resolution and was finally struck through a year later. In fact, to admit a new, though limited, category of "electronic personality" – assuming that the matter can be considered within the general law-making competence of the EU – would have required a huge effort of conceptualization and harmonization of private law regulations within the legislations of the 27 EU member states. Moreover, beside the media interest in the innovation contained in the European Parliament document, the mentioned paragraph raised discontent among many observers, including experts and scholars in the fields of AI, philosophy, and law.

This concern was finally voiced in an open letter, circulated in April 2018,[162] where the subscribers, having premised the quite obvious consideration that "legal status for a robot can't derive from the natural person model", added that

160 Quoted fn. 1.

161 See Klaus J. Hopt, "Comparative Company Law", Mathias Reimann and Reinhard Zimmermann (eds.) *The Oxford Handbook of Comparative Law*, Oxford: OUP, 2006.

162 https://g8fip1kplyr33r3krz5b97d1-wpengine.netdna-ssl.com/wp-content/uploads/2018/04/RoboticsOpenLetter.pdf.

> legal status for a robot can't derive from the *legal entity* model, since it implies the existence of human persons behind the legal person to represent and direct it. And this is not the case for a robot.

Legal status for a robot, finally – in the opinion of those who signed the open letter – could not derive from the common law *Trust model* (also arranged as *Fiducie* or *Treuhand* in continental Europe), as

> it would still imply the existence of a human being as a last resort – the trustee or fiduciary – responsible for managing the robot granted with a *Trust* or a *Fiducie*.[163]

As a result, an amendment for par. 59f. was listed and 285 Members of the European Parliament voted in favor of its deletion.

What this story tells us is that the traditional paradigm based on the presence of the human being "behind" the action of legal entities and corporations still holds as the main reason to validate the legal fiction of legal personality for corporate entities.

Later on (February 12, 2019) the European Parliament adopted a Resolution on a comprehensive European industrial policy on artificial intelligence and robotics.[164] After describing AI as "one of the strategic technologies of the 21st century", the European Parliament presented several recommendations to the Member States, advocating "a human-centric technology," which would avoid possible misuses of AI technologies to the detriment of people's fundamental rights. Through the Resolution, the European Parliament insisted on the predominance of the human factor over computer systems, which is based on "the 'man operates machine' principle of responsibility," and recommends that "humans must always be ultimately responsible for decision-making".[165]

---

163 See Stathis Banakas, "Understanding Trusts: A Comparative View of Property Rights in Europe", *Indret*, 1, 2006, p. 323.

164 2018/2088 (INI).

165 Ibid.

5 "If a Machine Acts as Intelligently as a Human Being Then It Is as Intelligent as a Human Being"[166]

Copyright law requires that, to be protected, a work must be original. Authorship cannot be examined in isolation, since the requirement of *originality* is correlative:[167] a work must have been developed by its author.[168] An originality test denotes the other side of the authorship coin, as it reflects the idea that, to be original, an artwork requires an author. This is another aspect of the difficulties experienced by classic law when dealing with AI-Generated Art.

In fact, neither the Berne convention nor other international regulations provide a description of "originality".[169] Undefined, the term goes along with a wide-ranging number of vague notions[170] that are used in the drafting of international conventions. Since 1886 the UCB has remained silent on the notion of originality, leaving its determination to local regulators and judicial decisions. It is, then, possible that the same artwork may not be equally protected in the different countries that signed the UCB.[171]

Local legal diversities in the definition of this standard have serious consequences for the copyright system:

> if the standards for a work to be considered original, and thus qualify for copyright protection, are raised or lowered, both the number and types

166 Alan Turing, *Computer Machinery and Intelligence*, *Mind* October 1950, p. 433.

167 Jane Ginsburg, "The Concept of Authorship in Comparative Copyright Law", 52 *De Paul L. Rev.* 2003, 1063, p. 1077.

168 In copyright law "originality" is not identical to the "novelty" requirement for patent protection. Originality refers to "coming from someone as the originator/author", rather than "never having occurred before".

169 Diplomatic records confirm that this requirement was not included in the Berne Convention as it was considered to be evident. See James Koessler, "Something for Nothing? The Standard of 'Originality' in Copyright Law", *SSRN Papers*, (December 28, 2012), p. 2. The Berne Convention defines the scope of protection also by stating that "Encyclopedias and anthologies which, by reason of the selection and arrangement of their contents constitute intellectual creations shall be protected as such", thus implying that this is a threshold for originality (art. 2.5.).

170 See Gianmaria Ajani, "Ruling by Indicators: How the Use of Vague Notions and Quantitative Indicators Facilitates Legal Change", 23 *Cardozo Electronic Law Bulletin*, 2017, 3–25.

171 In fact, originality standards are not harmonized globally. Not only might there be different standards for different categories of works within a country (e.g., computer programs, databases, and photographs may have a distinct standard from other works), but different countries might apply the same standard differently in the judicial practice (consider, e.g., the more rigorous application of the personality test in Germany).

> of works that can claim copyright protection will change. Thus, what is at stake in any definition or redefinition of originality is the coverage of the copyright monopoly and the balance between copyright owners and users at its most basic level.[172]

The rigidity of taxonomies contained in most copyright regulations made it possible to maintain the originality standard very low.[173] As long as grouping by genres – like painting, sculpture, and so forth – was used to solve almost any query on the "what" of art, there was no need to use originality as a severe criterion to tell what art is protectable and what is not.

And here we find an interesting trait of originality: its wavering between subjectivism and objectivism. When discussing authorship, I observed a swinging between the subject\author, as the center of any definition of authorship, and the object\artwork, as the element that gives the author their status. Likewise, two schools of thought have parted the definition of originality in copyright law. The first, called objectivist, defines originality as something resulting from "skill and labor".[174] The second, called subjectivist, characterizing France and the French-inspired civil law systems, refuses "skill and labor" as a prime

172 Howard B. Abrams, "Originality and Creativity in Copyright Law", 55 *Law and Contemporary Problems*, 1992, 3–44, p. 3.

173 Annemarie Bridy, quoted fn. 11.

174 Traditionally, British law defines a work as "original" when it results from the "skill and labor" of its author. This line of reasoning was followed for several decades in the jurisdictions of Australia, Canada and in the United States, until the Feist case (*Feist Pub., Inc. v. Rural Tel. Serv. Co.*, 499 U.S. (1991) 340) established that a telephone book cannot be protected under Copyright law, "if the listing of the data is not creative in any way". The court opinion stated that copyright protection could only be granted to "works of authorship" that possess "*at least some* minimal degree of creativity".

Under Canadian copyright law, to be eligible for protection a work must be *original to its author*, not copied from another work, and requires more than trivial or mechanical intellectual effort. In the case of *CCH Canadian Ltd. v. Law Society of Upper Canada*, the Supreme Court of Canada examined the different approaches taken to the definition of originality. The Supreme Court ultimately concluded that the proper approach in Canadian law falls between the approach of labor and diligence, and that of creativity.

Germany is somehow different. Although the standard may not be different, German courts have applied a stricter test. Influenced by Kantian theories, which linked creative expression with the formation and deployment of personal autonomy and, therefore, attached great importance to artistic expression, modern German doctrine combines a mostly subjective search for individuality (*Individualitiät*) with the requirement of a minimal threshold of creativity (*Gestaltungshöhe*).

requisite for copyright, opting instead for a mark of the "author's personality" in the work.[175]

This historical diversity between the Anglo-American concept and the Continental one still affects the legal standards, and the vagueness about the degree of originality causes diverging interpretations also with regard to AI-generated artworks.[176] We can observe one side the attempt – introduced by British law – to identify as the author a person who had a role in "undertaking the necessary arrangements" to obtain the given outcome;[177] on the other, within continental law, the remains of the ancient connection between originality and author's personality. Both hinder a possible identification of AI-autonomously produced work as authored by the machine. This also explains, I believe, the (so far, failed) attempt by the European Parliament to overcome the dilemma by introducing a new concept of "digital personhood".

How, then, can one find the "personality" of the author in a "creative machine"? In fact, similar questions appeared in case law long before the last generation of AI-driven systems began to challenge authorship. Somehow, EU and civil law national regulations[178] adjusted to new technologies not by changing their patterns – still based on the search for the mark of the author's personality – but rather by reducing the significance of the originality standard and adding a "modicum of creativity". This conveyed a doctrine of *creative*

---

175 This condition sees the work as an emanation of its (human) creator. *Art. 112–1* of the French "*Code de la propriété intellectuelle*" establishes that "Les dispositions du présent code protègent les droits des auteurs sur toutes les oeuvres de l'esprit, quels qu'en soient le genre, la forme d'expression, le mérite ou la destination". "L'originalité est l'empreinte de la personnalité de l'auteur", Cour d'Appel de Paris, 1er avril 1957, D. 1957–436. For a clear rejection, within French law, of the "labor and skill" principle, see Cass. 1e civ., May 2, 1989 JCP G 1990, II, 21392, noted by André Lucas, *Rev. Int. Droit Aut.* 1990, p. 309.

176 In cases of AIartworks, each *oeuvre* is distinctive. This does not mean, however, that it is original for the purpose of copyright law, as the courts have interpreted the concept of originality as "originating from the author."

177 See *supra* fn. 115.

178 "Without harmonisation at Community level, legislative activities at national level which have already been initiated in a number of Member States in order to respond to the technological challenges might result in significant differences in protection and thereby in restrictions on the free movement of services and products incorporating, or based on, intellectual property, leading to a refragmentation of the internal market and legislative inconsistency"; see the Directive 2001/29/EC "On the harmonization of certain aspects of copyright and related rights in the information society" (Preamble, no. 6). These arguments were made with regard to the developments of technology faced by European societies at the beginning of the 21st century but are also valid for the developments and challenges we face today with respect to artificial intelligence.

choices quite similar to the minimal test pronounced in the U.S. *Feist vs. Rural* case.[179]

It is interesting to note how judges have adapted the requirement of copyright protection based on "originality" to the changing technological conditions. Their action was needed because neither the European subjective factor, linked to the personality of the author, nor the Anglo-American objective feature (labor and skill) were of use anymore to grasp the meaning of originality. Facing new reproductive techniques and a distancing of the author from the production of the artwork, courts added "a *minimal amount of creativity*" as a distinguishing element to make originality fit the new conditions. By doing this, judges moved the pendulum from the objective standard (originality as an identifiable *fact*, meaning "originated by the author") towards a rather subjective criterium: creativity.[180]

A revealing example of the transformation of the standard is the *Painer* case in the EU Court of Justice.[181] The Court in Luxembourg ruled that a photo is "original" if the photographer "was able to express his creative abilities in the production of the work by making free and creative choices". The Court also explained that when a photographer engages in portrait photography, they have many creative choices at their disposal, such as choosing the background, the pose, the framing, the light, as well as printing and editing techniques. This

179 Following *Feist vs. Rural*, the term "original", as it is used in copyright, means only that a work is independently created by the author (as opposed to copied from other works), and that "it possesses at least some minimal degree of creativity". *Feist Pub. Inc. v. Rural Tel. Serv. Co.*, 499 U.S. (1991) 340, p. 345.

Like many other commentators, Michael Madison contended that the creativity standard has become so empty after *Feist*, that it would be more productive to put it aside, focusing instead on copyright as a mechanism for producing and disseminating knowledge. Asserting that "creativity has exhausted itself conceptually" as an anchor for copyright law, Madison advocates the re-conceptualization of copyright as "knowledge law." Michael J. Madison, "Beyond Creativity: Copyright as Knowledge Law", 12 *Vand. J. Ent. & Tech. L.* 2010, p. 817.

180 In the EU, the Computer Programs Directive (2009/24) states that a computer program "shall be protected if it is original in the sense that it is the *author's own intellectual creation.* No other criteria shall be applied to determine its eligibility for protection" (art. 1.3.). The Database Directive (1996/9) provides that "databases which, by reason of the selection or arrangement of their contents, constitute the author's own intellectual creation shall be protected as such by copyright and no other criteria shall be applied to determine their eligibility for that protection" (art. 3.1.).

In the Murphy case (2011) the European Court of Justice ruled that the creative process must leave room for "creative freedom". This implies that a creative output has to be the result of at least some intentionality from the author.

181 C-145/10.

is why "by making those various choices, the author of a portrait photograph can stamp the work created with his 'personal touch'".[182]

If the definition of creativity proves to be problematic in classic copyright law, one can expect it to be more than challenging when applied to AI-art. Scholars from different disciplines have been debating the role of "creativity in machines" already since the 1960s.[183] The new generation of AI autonomous systems has revived the discussion. These systems cannot be identified as mere objects, used for making other items. It is the capacity to operate creatively that, as we have seen above, differentiates AI from other tools. However, the discussion on creativity is bound to remain unsolved, as there is no common definition of what creativity means, not only when applied to computers, but also to human beings.[184]

We have seen above how the split between the legal world and the art world on the matter of authorship can cause different answers to the question: "Who is the author?". Now, how does the standard of "originality + creative choice" match the reality of AI-generated artwork? Is the notion of creativity necessarily linked to a "human factor", or can we conceive an AI-made work as an output resulting from a (human, or non-human) "choice"? Again, answers very, depending on how we define "the modicum of creativity" in the process of decision making.

Legal practice defines creativity as an author's innovative choice that is not *dictated* by the function of the work, the method or technique used, or by applicable standards or relevant good practice.[185] As we have seen, AI-generated works are the outcome of computations whose results cannot be foreseen by programmers; today:

> the whole essence of AI is that the way in which it reacts will not be capable of prediction. Just like the human brain, its response will be governed not simply by the program but by its interpretation of the program and the stimuli.[186]

182 http://curia.europa.eu/juris/liste.jsf?&num=C-145/10.

183 Calvin W. Taylor has recorded over fifty definitions of creativity in the literature from the 1960s onwards. Quoted by David Levy, *Robots Unlimited: Life in A Virtual Age* AK Peters: Natick MA, 2006, p. 149.

184 See Jan Zibner, "Artificial Intelligence: A Creative Player in the Game of Copyright" 10 *Eur. J. of L. & Tech.*, 2019, 1–16.

185 Dennis Karjala, 15 UCLA *Entertainment L. R.* 2008, 169, p. 182.

186 Colin Davies quoted fn. 24, p. 614.

Those works are, undeniably, original, both in their making and in their outcome, as they do not represent a copy of other works. The question is whether the creativity requirement applies or not. Again, we are at a crossway between the legal world, where the human factor in creativity still counts, and the art world, where creativity can be also ascribed to machines.

The legal discourse, as articulated in case law, links the presence of creativity to an "innate, hard-to-define aesthetic sensibility that is particular to living creatures",[187] as it would implicate consciousness and, ultimately, the presence of an *idea*. Following this conventional approach, one has to conclude that advanced technology systems, such as AI, which are capable of creating independent and original works, do not satisfy the requirement of creativity, even though the law's requirement is minimal.

We cannot avoid, therefore, going back to what we have already seen when we approached the authorship issue: lack of creativity – as it has been articulated by the law and in judicial cases – means lack of copyright protection. Defining creativity in terms of "human consciousness" sets a standard that, by definition, intelligent machines will never be able to reach.

Still, one could cultivate proposals on the nature of "strong AI creativity".[188] Research on Artificial Intelligence follows two different lines: "strong AI" and "weak AI". Experts on "weak AI" claim it will only be able to operate machines that *seem* to be intelligent. Those promoting a "strong AI" contend that artificial intelligence will be able to do whatever is within the capacity of weak AI and also develop a consciousness, thanks to its increasing capacity to autonomously understand things from its surroundings.

Additionally, if neuroscience researchers argue that all creativity, including the human kind, is inherently algorithmic,[189] should we not say that works produced autonomously by computers are more related to existing copyright doctrines than appearances may at first suggest?

Italo Calvino, one of the most important Italian fiction writers of the 20th century, was not only provocative when he argued that "writers, as they have always been up to now, are already writing machines".[190]

> Avant-gardists like Calvino raise the possibility that humans and machines, if we consider the rule-bound nature of their respective outputs

187 Keith Sawyer, *Explaining Creativity: The Science of Human Innovation*, Oxford: OUP, 2014, p. 29.

188 See Vishnu Nath, Stephen Levinson *Autonomous Robotics and Deep Learning*, New York: Springer 2014, p. 2.

189 See Anna Abraham, *The Neuroscience of Creativity*, Cambridge: CUP, 2018.

190 Italo Calvino, quoted fn. 5, p. 10.

> and the pre-existing models they are wont to emulate, are really not as different as we are conditioned to believe.[191]

As in a set of Russian dolls, the human factor re-emerges from every notion, be it authorship, originality or creativity. Being rooted into classic copyright law, it pulls like a magnet any possible interpretation internal to the legal discourse. In fact, a strong argument to deny authorship to AI systems lies in the basic presupposition of all copyright laws, namely the idea-expression dichotomy, which stipulates that copyright protects expressions of ideas and not ideas as such.

We must, therefore, accept that the legal world is not ready to abandon its classical setup. However, as for the notion of *author*, new elaborations on the concept of creativity occur outside of the legal world. For example, a cognitive revolution in psychology led scholars to identify different patterns of creativity, depending on the complexity of the processes, and to uphold that creativity never occurs in isolation.[192] This is not to deny that much of good art is still made by lone artists, who act on the basis of pure sentiment and have no interest in connecting with a context or an audience. Their action is, and with good reason remains, covered by classic copyright laws.

We should, however, recognize that classic law is crippled by the advancement of new technologies, and in particular by the new AI-autonomously generated *oeuvres*. This might eventually lead the legal world to be inspired by the art world, so as to improve its connection with those technologies.

As said, countless descriptions have been associated with the concept of "creativity": one may find thoughts upon "weak" or "strong", "exploratory" or "transformational", as well as "4th dimensional" creativity. The model of creativity devised by Mihaly Csikszentmihalyi[193] includes three interrelated elements:

- an accepted, and agreed upon, domain of current knowledge;
- an agent who alters a component of the domain to produce something novel; and
- a field of experts that ultimately decides whether or not the novelty will be accepted into the existing domain.

---

191 Annemarie Bridy quoted fn. 9 p. 11.

192 Daniel Gruner and Mihaly Csikszentmihalyi, quoted fn. 14, p. 447.

193 Mihaly Csikszentmihalyi, "Society, culture, and person: A systems view of creativity" in Robert Sternberg (ed.), *The Nature of Creativity: Contemporary Psychological Perspectives*, Cambridge: CUP 1988, 325–339.

Looking for conditions under which an agent may be perceived as creative, Kyle Jennings has identified three criteria to be met in order to qualify a system as featuring creative autonomy:

- "autonomous evaluation (the system can evaluate its liking of a creation without seeking opinions from an outside source);[194]
- autonomous change (the system initiates and guides changes to its standards without being explicitly directed when and how to do so);
- non-randomness (the system's evaluations and standard changes are not purely random)".[195]

Applying these criteria to AI means that

> to progress from a capable apprentice to a creator in its own right, an AI system must be able to both independently apply and independently change the standards it uses. This ideal will be called 'creative autonomy,' and represents the system's freedom to pursue a course independent of its programmer's or operator's intentions.[196]

Following these approaches, an author is not the only component of the creative process. Nor does creativity exist independently in any of the listed elements. Rather, creativity depends on individual capacity, acquisition of information and judgment by experts.[197]

This perspective can free AI-systems from the identification of "autonomy" as a state of complete segregation. In fact, Kyle Jennings has a good argument in supporting the recognition of a truly independent AI system as one where transformational (and not pure exploratory) creativity emerges out of interactions among many different agents: "in such an environment, machine learning technique may enable an AI system to change its preferences not randomly, but as a reaction to continuously collected evaluations and opinions".[198] Also, an AI system may attain experience from the senses: projects with AI painters

194 Following definitions provided by Kyke Jennings (quoted *infra* fn. 194) "autonomous evaluation requires that the system be able to issue opinions without consulting an outside human or machine intelligence. However, the system is free to ask for or observe others' opinions at other times, and to store this information".

195 Kyle E. Jennings "Developing Creativity: Artificial Barriers in Artificial Intelligence", 20 *Minds & Machines*, 2010, 489–501, p. 490.

196 Ibid.

197 Ibid.

198 Kyle Jennings quoted *supra* fn. 196, p. 499. However, he also says, "The system described here only makes changes in (possibly indirect) reaction to others' changes. Human creators, in contrast, proactively change their standards. It is conceivable that this system could make proactive changes by looking for patterns in how others' standards change

showed that AI paintings can be influenced by sounds, lights and temperature in the environment, or even keywords that the system autonomously chooses.[199]

Against the recurrent identification of the author as the one and only master of a creative process, Keith Sawyer also worked out a theory grounded on the socio-cultural definition of creativity. In his terms "creativity is the generation of a product that is judged to be novel and to be appropriate, useful, or valuable by a suitably knowledgeable social group".[200] This theory leads us back to the concept of an audience "contributing" to the completion of authorship.

Sawyer's theory of creativity as a cooperative action can have an impact on the notion of authorship: most of the programmers who create the algorithms for computational art are not artists themselves; they do not need to be poets or painters or writers. Nevertheless, they produce an artefact that generates art. Therefore,

> the programmer gets engaged in a creative process to create these algorithms that mimic the art production of a human artist. The process of AI art requires a combination of two different concepts that come together and generate something new. These two different concepts, art and computational systems, come together in the computational art (or AI art), as a new concept.[201]

The counterargument is well known: it can be summarized as follows: "it is not the machine's creativity at work, but the programmer's. While refusing the creative role of the machine, mainly suggest that a machine is not conscious, so it does not have desires, preferences or values to appreciate or judge what it is doing".

with time and in relation to each other, which would be proactive, though perhaps *not purposeful enough* to be considered creative" [emphasis added].

199 Richard Moss "Creative AI: the robots that would be painters" https://newatlas.com/creative-ai-algorithmic-art-painting-fool-aaron/36106/.

200 Ibid, p. 8, as quoted by Deniz Kurt fn. 141, p. 52.

201 Ibid.

However, as Margaret Boden points out

> this would be an underestimation: even though it is assumed that computers cannot be intentionally creative, it does not mean that artistic creativity of AI can be firmly excluded.[202]

Boden's position deserves attention: refusing to qualify as "art" AI-made works on the grounds of lack of creativity – this is her argument – seems to be too easy, and therefore fallacious, a point. It is, indeed, obvious that computers "do not have the intention to express an aesthetical or socio-political stance" because they do not have emotions or aesthetic taste. It is equally evident that computers "do not have an intention to express their feelings or to enunciate their thoughts as the human mind".[203] However, these perspectives would be limited by embracing a traditional notion of creativity as purely human, thereby constricting the search of what is new in AI-made art within a circular path, where authorship, originality and creativity are fused together in the inescapable "human factor". This might cause an undervaluation of AI-made art as a genre.

Quite paradoxically, the standard applied by traditional copyright law to AI-generated artworks is even tighter than what is already experienced in the context of contemporary art. Somehow, the practice of the legal world when dealing with many artists' challenges – such as creative randomized choices,[204] instructed actions,[205] or the fading of intentionality in art-making[206] – has not favored a transfer of knowledge in the case of managing AI-made art. The reason, it seems to me, lies in the following: deficiencies of classic copyright law

202 Margaret Boden, quoted, fn. 57, p. 7. See also Graeme Ritchie, "Some Empirical Criteria for Attributing Creativity to A Computer Program", 17 *Minds and Machines* 2007, 67–99. See also Christine Charyton "Art, Creativity, and Culture: How Art Intersects with Science in the Expression of Artistic Creativity", in Christine Charyton (ed.) *Creativity and Innovation Among Science and Art*, London: Springer, 179–204.

203 Deniz Kurt quoted *supra* fn. 141, p. 27.

204 Making art by randomness: this is a debated argument between those contesting the possibility of machine-creativity (their argument being that randomness, producing coincidental *oeuvres*, does not require an intentional action, as the distribution of outcomes can be easily be set before the program starts), and those minimizing the diversities between human intelligence and AI (claiming that many artist, like Pollock or Richter, used randomness as a way to flash out their creativity).

205 See, for example, Whitney Frank, "Instructions for Destruction: Yoko Ono's Performance Art", *intersections* 10, 1, 2009, 571–607.

206 See, for instance, works by artist James Deller, whose research is about "losing control of his artistic authorship". Or the "Community projects" made in Chicago by the artist Theaster Gates.

regarding conceptual art have been compensated for by (human) authors who found alternative legal instruments to protect their work.

Hence the variety of agreements, imposed contracts, deeds and certificates elaborated throughout the years to provide legal protection. Somehow, artists interested in doing this (Yves Klein, Daniel Buren, Edward Kienholz, Sol Lewitt and, more recently, Maria Eichhorn, Carey Young) act as "private legislators".[207] While downgrading the importance of the artwork\object and emphasizing the *process* or human relations, artists maintained and underlined their capacity to produce valid alternative legal frames. Freedom of contracting has, indeed, played an important role in supplying tailor-made solutions to *authors without (material) works*.

There is not, however, a situation comparable to *AIworks without authors*. Whenever *oeuvres* are not given voice by their authors, or protection by the general interest (i.e., the law), they remain orphans. Hence the difficult and, ultimately, unfertile search for alternatives based on existing copyright law.

6 Conclusion: "Art Makes Meaning"[208]

The definition of what art is must be found within the process of making and experiencing artworks. Over time, this assertion took on diverse modes; in certain contexts, the decision on what art is falls within the art world. Others also have a say on art, like telling what is authentic or forged, tradeable or not. These qualifications, however, spell out technical variations about what has been already categorized by and within the art world.

The legal world has the authority to provide protection to artists while considering the public interest, not to tell what art is and what it is not. Even when it classifies art genres, as copyright laws and regulations giving privileges for fiscal reasons do, the law does not rule on artistic values.

There is no need to provide evidence that art is considered intrinsically valuable by all legal systems in the world, and it therefore has to be legally protected and promoted. However, most legal systems in the world are tongue-tied when it comes to providing a definition of *what* art is. Even if lawyers generally

207 See Daniel McLean, "Authenticity in Art and Law: A Question of Attribution or Authorization?" in Susan Hapgood and Cornelia Lauf, *In Deed: Certificates of Authenticity in Art*, Amsterdam: Roma Pub. 2011, 88–96.

208 Artist Joseph Kosuth said "art makes meaning"; in his work he investigated the ways in which art-making is tied to language. See Stuart Morgan, "Art as Idea as Idea. An interview with Joseph Kosuth", 16 *Frieze*, May 1994. I find this quote demonstrative of the capacity of the art world to qualify what art is.

believe that whatever deserves protection by the law must be identified and defined, when talking about law and art we are inclined to affirm that abstention from definition is a good thing:

> It would be a dangerous undertaking for judges, who are trained only to the law, to constitute themselves final judges of the worth of pictorial illustrations, outside of the narrowest and most obvious limits.[209]

This dated and renowned saying by Justice Oliver Holmes concisely voices the difficult search for a balance between the prescriptive elements contained in the law and a reality of arts that are as inconstant as they are unpredictable.[210]

A first break in the classical canon that, throughout the entire 19th century, had governed relationships between the law and the arts occurred more than a century ago. Since then, to bridge the gap between the two worlds, several connecting strategies had been elaborated, like:

- expanding the classification of genres adopted by international and national copyrights laws;
- providing protection to dematerialized art and its makers via the use of contracts;
- amending laws and regulations by *ad hoc* adjustments to protect software.

Advancements in technology and the latest generation of autonomous AI are posing a new challenge: neither interpretation nor simple adjustments of existing laws seem to be a proper response. For the first time we are experiencing a manner of making art which assumes the non-existence of a human author. Lacking an adequate understanding of the scale and perspectives of these advancements, it is likely that, while the art world is embracing AI-generated artworks, the legal world will still remain unresponsive.

This essay aimed to offer an overview of the phenomenon of AI-made art, and to observe how it could possibly be accommodated within the legal world. In so doing, I have distinguished between different kinds of AI-generated *oeuvres*. Some cases, to be accurate, do not really challenge current laws: whenever a human intervention can be detected in the creative process, the AI system

209 Bleistein v. Donaldson Lithographing Company, 188 U.S. 239 (1903), p. 251.

210 According to Christine Farley, however, "because judges are admonished never to make aesthetic determinations, they are forced to find other ways of deciding cases. Consequently, these disguised aesthetic judgments play havoc with the doctrines of law. Moreover, this ruse masks unexamined aesthetic determinations and thus biases and predilections. It would be preferable for judges to be explicit and self-conscious about their philosophical bent in making these determinations"; Christine Farley "Judging Art", 79 *Tulane Law Review* 2005, p. 805.

remains a tool – a sophisticated tool, but a tool nonetheless. And according to existing copyright laws, even a modest contribution is sufficient to recognize originality. An analogous solution applies whenever the artwork is independently created by the AI, but the human intervention consists in a selection of what is considerable for dissemination: here the law is clear in recognizing human authorship, as the act of selecting and choosing is traditionally considered copyrightable.

Beyond those instances, a remaining issue is whether a work *autonomously* generated and selected by an AI program, lacking any human involvement whatsoever, can be copyrighted. In this case, different arguments lead to the same conclusion: the current law is not satisfying. Yet lack of regulation does not necessarily go with a lack of qualification of the work as an artwork. It rather means absence of legal protection. To make up for this deficiency, several authors, from different research fields, have elaborated many proposals.

The first one, as we have seen, stems from the same structure of copyright laws: works without protection fall into a regime of public domain. This, of course, should not affect works jointly made by human *and* AI. AI-independently made works in the public domain will be available for free use. However, identifying authorship in the case of works crafted by an indistinct merging of human and machine contributions might prove to be problematic. This would lead to a detrimental uncertainty in the legal protection of those instances; also, one can imagine potential conflicts between individuals claiming authorial rights on the artwork and other parties, interested in having the public domain recognized in court.

And while the default solution based on the public domain could hold within civil law countries, it would be quite critical in those common law jurisdictions where regulations based on the legal fiction of "the person making the arrangements for the work" have been enacted.[211] This would determine an unfortunate diversity between the continental and the common law jurisdictions on the treatment of AI-made works.

Other conflictual situations based on the principle of non-discrimination in copyright law could arise whenever a person holding an interest in an AI-generated artwork would contend that a work of art created by an AI system and not distinguishable from one made by a human should receive protection. The decision of the court in such a case would depend on the approach to the concept of originality adopted. The supposed simplicity of the "public domain option" would not stand up to those reservations.

211 See fn. 115.

Other legal mechanisms devised by some commentators (like the extension of the "work made for hire" doctrine, or the extension of the norms on protection of "previously unpublished works")[212] share, in my opinion, a critical point: they are all based on fragile legal fictions, being the adjustment of models originally intended for completely different situations. Also, they cannot easily be transplanted from a common law environment into a civil law legal order.

Those who are not persuaded by the public domain option, nor by thorny adjustments of current regulations, could consider a set of different solutions integrated by the method of allocating rights to individuals playing a role in the AI process (programmer, user). As mentioned, those solutions also suffer from serious uncertainties on the actual determination of personal contributions.

We are finally left with the most radical option: to recognize to AI-generative systems an entitlement to their autonomously produced artworks *de lege ferenda*. While this would be in line with some projects already developed and accepted by the art world, from a purely legal perspective such a proposal would entail not only a technical, but also a "cultural revolution" within classical copyright law. This is not to deny that the time to rethink classical copyright law has come; rather, we should recognize that vesting AI systems with a sort of legal personhood is not a minor action to be taken, as it implies legal changes in other areas of the law and not only in copyright regulations.

The existence of autonomous AI processes is today a fact. As such it deserves improved attention and needs, in my opinion, to be treated in the framework of the wider debate on a future "law of robots". So far, within the art world, various actions have been taken in the direction of calling "author" an independent and creative AI system. During the 20th century, the art world's actors (artists and curators, dealers and critics) set the spotlight on the "*what*-in-art" and gave *aura* to items that the legal world was not ready to consider to be artistic, such as promises, instructions, words. Today, part of the art world is embracing cases where *the work is in search of a (non-human) author*. In an attempt to make up for the absence of a human factor on the authorial side, some swing the focus from the author's feeling to the sentiment experienced by the audience.

---

212 Directive 2006/116 "On the term of protection of copyright and certain related rights", art. 4: "*Protection of previously unpublished works*. Any person who, after the expiry of copyright protection, for the first time lawfully publishes or lawfully communicates to the public a previously unpublished work, shall benefit from a protection equivalent to the economic rights of the author. The term of protection of such rights shall be 25 years from the time when the work was first lawfully published or lawfully communicated to the public".

Art production is not detached from the technological process;[213] it has never been, from the time when painters experienced new ways to make pastels, to the invention of cameras and videos. The coming of AI-driven agents cannot be treated as a simple quantitative upgrade in technology, as it affects the core of the relationship between art and law: authorship and originality. This is what the art world is saying to legislators and policy makers. Some timid moves can be noticed on the part of policy makers; one was the (so far, failed) invitation by the EU Parliament to the Commission to design a legal frame for assigning a limited personhood to AI systems. The lack of success of that attempt reveals that, at least in Europe, policy makers are far from being convinced about the necessity to provide a functional and adaptive legal "housing" for the various types of artificial intelligence. Still, the case should be reconsidered at the EU level, to prevent further diversity among national legal orders.

In my view, the case of authorship in AI autonomously generated art – already considered by the art world – should find its way within the larger frame of the law of (and for) robots. In the meantime, rather than developing fragile legal fictions, built on some elements of company or copyright laws that have been designed for different aims, the legal world should develop contractual models.

Whenever the current law does not fit the needs of our human communities, contracts have proven to be the most adaptable, flexible and specific remedy to gaps in legislation. Agreements could determine, case by case, how to allocate privileges and rights, how to distinguish the contribution of every participant. And whenever no human involvement in the art creation is detectable, contracts will be giving legal significance to the inventiveness of the AI designers, and to the art world's openness to the disappearance of the human author.

In Europe, a proactive role in adapting the law of contracts to a profound change in market relations has been played by scholars and experts, judicial courts, and EU institutions. As a result, new areas of conventional relationships have been established, mostly based on agreed commitments to share rights and allocate privileges, so as to increase information for the benefit of the parties involved and the general public. Those efforts share a common trait, namely the overcoming of the rigidity of the classical contract of sale and of its boundaries, tightly influenced by property laws.

---

213 See Maurizio Ferraris "From Fountain to Moleskine. The Work of Art in the Age of Its Technological Producibility", 2.4 *Art and Law*, (4) 2019, Leiden Boston: Brill, p. 5ff.

The art world is said not to have a good disposition toward contracting and whatever it involves.[214] This is certainly true. AI-generated art, however, occurs within a different environment, where know-how and financial investments in technology favor peculiar attitudes toward the recourse to voluntary agreements. Contracts and agreements among "non-authors" could provide some predictability, while waiting for the law to receive and possibly regulate the creative inputs provided by the art world. To reach that point, however, a cultural change is needed: a change that innovators in art-generating AI cannot attain on their own, but that will eventually be caused by more robust policy concerns prompted by advancements in robots' capacity to sense, to think, and to act.

Acknowledgments

The author wishes to thank the Käte Hamburger Kolleg "Recht als Kultur", in Bonn, where he was hosted as a Fellow from October 2019 to March 2020. The multidisciplinary spirit which inspires the Centre has been a great intellectual inspiration in the writing of this essay. He is grateful to Werner Gephart, to Maria Eichhorn and to Carey Young for their insights on the research matter. Special thanks are due also to Andrea Baldini, Barbara Pasa and Filippo Vindrola for their competent and smart comments on the first draft.

Bibliography

Abbott Ryan, "I Think, Therefore I Invent: Creative Computers and the Future of Patent Law", 57 *Brit.Col. L. Rev.* 2016, 1079.

Abraham Anna, *The Neuroscience of Creativity*, Cambridge: CUP, 2018.

Abrams Howard B., "Originality and Creativity in Copyright Law", 55 *Law and Contemporary Problems* 1992, 3–44.

214 John Merryman rightly noted: "In the art world, the word "contract" is a red flag. People react emotionally and irrationally to it. A common statement by artists and dealers about contracts is: 'I don't want (need?) a contract with my dealer (artist?)'. This is foolish, because where there is an artist dealer relationship there is a contract. It is just that the contract is implied rather than expressed, that is fragmentary, rather than comprehensive, that its terms are supplied by a legal system that is not art world wise, rather than by the artist and gallery concerned", *Law, Ethics and the Visual Arts* (John Henry Merryman, Albert E. Elsen, Stephen K. Urice eds.) Alphen a/d Rijn: Kluwer, 5th ed., 2007, p. 852.

Ajani Gianmaria, "Ruling by Indicators: How the Use of Vague Notions and Quantitative Indicators Facilitates Legal Change", 23 *Cardozo Electronic Law Bulletin*, 2017, 3–25.

Andina Tiziana, "What is Art? The Question of Definition Reloaded", 1.2 *Art and Law* 2017, Leiden, Boston: Brill, 1–88.

Baldini Andrea, "Identity and Interpretation of Public Artworks: A Challenge to Intentionalism.", in 8 *Kultura-Społeczeństwo-Edukacja* 2015, 9–26.

Banakas Stathis, "Understanding Trusts: A Comparative View of Property Rights in Europe", *Indret*, 2006, 323.

Barron Anne, "Copyright Law and the Claim of Arts", 4 *Intellectual Property Quarterly*, 2002, 384.

Boden Margaret, *The Creative Mind: Myths and Mechanisms*, Routledge: New York, 2004.

Boden Margaret and Edmonds Ernest A., "What is Generative Art?" 2009, 20 *Digital Creativity*, 1.

Bonadio Enrico and Lucchi Nicola (eds.), *Non-Conventional Copyright. Do New and Non-Traditional Works Deserve Protection?"* Elgar: London, 2018.

Bostrom Nick, "How Long Before Superintelligence", 2 *Int. J. Future Stud.* 1998.

Bridy Annemarie, "Fearless Girl Meets Charging Bull: Copyright and the Regulation of Intertextuality", 9 *UC Irvine Law Review*, 2019.

Bridy Annemarie, "Coding Creativity: Copyright and the Artificially Intelligent Author", 5 *Stan. Tech. L. Rev*. 2012.

Brown Mark, "New Rembrandt to be Unveiled in Amsterdam", *The Guardian*, April 5, 2016.

Calvino Italo, *The Literature Machine. Essays*, 1980) (Patrick Craig transl.), New York: Random House, 1997.

Carpenter Megan and Hetcher Steven, "Function over Form: Bringing the Fixation Requirement into the Modern Era", 82 *Fordham L. Rev.* 2014, 2221–2271.

Carronn Louise, "Welcome to the Machine: Law, Artificial Intelligence and the Visual Arts", https://itsartlaw.org/2018/11/26/welcome-to-the-machine/.

Clifford Ralph D., "Intellectual Property in the Era of the Creative Computer Program: Will the True Creator Please Stand Up?", 71 *Tul. L. Rev*. 1997, 1675.

Condello Angela and Terrone Enrico, "Genre Classification: A Problem of Normativity and Exemplarity", in Gephart Werner and Leko Jure (eds.) *Law and the Arts. Elective Affinities and Relationships of Tension*, Frankfurt a./M.: Klostermann, 2017.

Craig Caris J. and Kerr Ian, "The Death of the AI Author" *Osgoode Legal Studies Research Paper* 2019.

Davies Colin R. "An Evolutionary Step in Intellectual Property Rights. Artificial Intelligence and Intellectual Property" 27 *Computer Law & Security Rev.* 2011, 601–619.

Deazley Ronan, Kretschmer Martin, Bently Lionel, *Privilege and Property. Essay on the History of Copyright*, Oxford: Open Books Pub., 2010.

Deleuze Gilles and Guattari Félix, *What is Philosophy*? New York: Columbia University Press, 1994.

Dickie George, *Art and Aesthetics. An Institutional Analysis,* Ithaca, NY: Cornell UP, 1974.

Donati Alessandra, *Law and Art: Diritto Civile e Arte Contemporanea,* Milan: Giuffré, 2012.

Duboff Leonard D., "Toward a Legal Definition of Art", 12 *Hastings Communication & Entertainment L.J.* 1990, 303.

Dziemidok Bohdan and McCornick Peter eds., *On the Aesthetics of Roman Ingarden: Interpretations and Assessments*, Kluwer: The Hague, 1989.

Ferraris Maurizio "From Fountain to Moleskine. The Work of Art in the Age of Its Technological Producibility", 2.4 *Art and Law*, 2019, Leiden, Boston: Brill, 1–87.

Fjeld Jessica and Mason Kortz, "A Legal Anatomy of AI-generated Art: Part I", *Harvard J. L. & Tech.*, November 2017, 1.

Floridi Luciano *The Fourth Revolution. How the Infosphere is Reshaping Human Reality*, Oxford: OUP, 2014.

Foucault Michel, *What Is an Author?*, in Paul Rabinow (ed.), *The Foucault Reader*, 1984, 101.

Galanter Philip, "XEPA: Intelligent Sculptures as Experimental Platforms for Computational Aesthetic Evaluation", 2013. www.philipgalanter.com.

Gaskin Sam, "When Art Created by Artificial Intelligence Sells, Who Gets Paid?", *Art Market*, September 17, 2018.

Gephart Werner, "Abstraction: A Myth of the Occidental World", Gephart Werner and Leko Jure (eds.), *Law and the Arts. Elective Affinities and Relationships of Tension*, Frankfurt a./M.: Klostermann, 2017, 291.

Ginsburg Jane, "People Not Machines: Authorship and What It Means in the Berne Convention" 49, *International Review of Intellectual Property and Competition Law* 2018, 131.

Ginsburg Jane, The Concept of Authorship in Comparative Copyright Law", 52 *De Paul L. Rev.* 2003, 1063.

Ginsburg Jane, "A Tale of Two Copyrights: Literary Property in Revolutionary France and America", 64 *Tul. L. Rev.* 1990, 99.

Goodfellow Ian J., Pouget-Abadie Jean, Mirza Mehdi, Bing Xu, Warde-Farley David, Ozair Sherjil, Courville Aaron, Bengio Yoshua, "Generative Adversarial Networks", *Advances in neural information processing systems*, 2014, 2672–2680.

Grimmelmann James, "There's No Such Thing as a Computer-Authored Work – And It's a Good Thing, Too", 39 *Colum. J. L. & Arts* 2016, 403.

Gruner Daniel and Csikszentmihalyi Mihaly, "Engineering Creativity in an Age of Artificial Intelligence", in Lebuda Isabela and Glaveanu Vlad Petre (eds.) *The Palgrave Handbook of Social Creativity Research*, Springer: Cham, 2019, 447.

Guadamuz Andres, "The Monkey Selfie: Copyright Lessons for Originality in Photographs and Internet Jurisdiction", *Internet Policy Review*, 2016, 5.

Hallevy Gabriel, "Unmanned vehicles. Subordination to criminal law under the modern concept of criminal liability" 21 *J. Law, Information & Soc.* 2011, 211.

Harman Graham, *Prince of Networks: Bruno Latour and Metaphysics,* Melbourne: re.Press, 2009.

Hodgkins Kelly, "A British artist spent 10 years teaching this robot how to draw, and it totally shows", *Digital Art*, (July 27, 2016).

Horvath Gizela, "The Rhetoric of Absence in Contemporary Art", Rozália Klára Bakó, Krisztina Bernáth, Éva Bíró Kaszás, Izabella Györgyjakab, Gizella Horváth (eds.) *Argumentor. Proceedings of the Second International Conference on Argumentation and Rhetoric*, Partiumi Kiadó, Oradea and Debrecen University Press, Debrecen, 2012, 175–195.

Hristov Kalin, "Artificial Intelligence and the Copyright Dilemma", 57 *IDEA: The IP Law Review,* 2017.

Hristov Kalin, "Artificial Intelligence and the Copyright Survey", JSPG, Vol. 16, Issue 1, April 2020, available at https://www.researchgate.net/publication/337387886_Artificial_Intelligence_and_the_Copyright_Survey/.

Huttunen Anniina, Ronkainen Anna, "Translation Technology and Copyright" *Nordic Intellectual Property Review* 2012, 330–344.

Jaszi Peter, "Toward a Theory of Copyright: The Metamorphoses of Authorship", *Duke L.J.* 1991, 455–505.

Jauk Emanuel, Benedek Mathias, Dunst Beate, Neubauer Aljoscha, "The relationship between intelligence and creativity: New support for the threshold hypothesis by means of empirical breakpoint detection", in 41 *Intelligence* (2013, July 4).

Julius Anthony, Quinn Malcolm, Schofield Philip (eds.), *Bentham and the Arts*, UCL Press: London, 2020.

Kalyanaraman Karthik, "AI Art: a New Photography Moment", https://medium.com/@info_12534/ai-art-a-new-photography moment-8d7009bfb696.

Kant Immanuel, The Metaphysics of Moral, 1797.

Koessler James, "Something for Nothing? The Standard of 'Originality' in Copyright Law", SSRN Papers, (December 28, 2012).

Krausz Michael, *Rightness and Reasons: Interpretation in Cultural Practices*, Cornell Univ. Press: Ithaca, 1993.

Kurt Deniz, *Artistic Creativity in Artificial Intelligence*, Nijmegen: Radboud Univ. 2018.

Langer Susanne K., *Feeling and Form: Theory of Art*, Routledge & Kegan, London, 1953.

Lebuda Isabela and Glaveanu Vlad Petre (eds.) *The Palgrave Handbook of Social Creativity Research.* Springer: Cham, 2019.

Lessig Lawrence, *Free Culture. How Big Media Uses Technology and the Law to Lock Down Culture and Control Creativity*, New York: Penguin Press, 2004.

Levy David, *Robots Unlimited: Life in A Virtual Age*, AK Peters: Natick MA, 2006.

Madison Michael J., "Beyond Creativity: Copyright as Knowledge Law", 12 *Vand. J. Ent. & Tech. L.* 2010, 817.

Maggiore Massimo, "Artificial Intelligence, computer generated works and copyright" in Bonadio Enrico and Lucchi Nicola, (eds.), *Non-Conventional Copyright* London: Elgar 2018, 382–400.

McCutcheon Jani "The vanishing author in computer-generated works: a critical analysis of recent Australian case law". 36 *Melbourne University Law Review* 2013 915–972.

McCutcheon Jani "Curing the authorless void: protecting computer generated works following Ice TV and Phone Directories", 37 *Melbourne University Law Review* 2013.

Merryman John Henry, Elsen Albert E., Urice Stephen K., (eds.) *Law, Ethics and the Visual Arts* Alphen a/d Rijn: Kluwer, 5th ed., 2007.

Mitchell Tom, *Machine Learning,* McGraw Hill series in Computer Sciences, New York: McGraw-Hill, 1997.

Morgan Stuart, "Art as Idea as Idea. An interview with Joseph Kosuth", 16 *Frieze*, May 1994.

Moss Richard, *Creative AI: The robots that would be painters.* 2015 http://newatlas.com/creative-ai-algorithmic-art-painting-fool-aaron/36106/.

Olowitz Chloe, "A Japanese A.I. program just wrote a short novel, and it almost won a literary prize", *Digital Trends*, March 23, 2016.

Pagallo Ugo, *The Law of Robots. Crime, Contracts and Torts*, Dordrecht: Springer 2013.

Pagallo Ugo, "As Law Goes By: Topology, Ontology, Evolution", in Pompeu Casanovas, Ugo Pagallo, Giovanni Sartor, Gianmaria Ajani, *AI Approaches to the Complexity of Legal Systems*, Dordrecht: Springer, 2010.

Pasa Barbara, "Industrial Design and Artistic Expression. The Challenge of Legal Protection" 4 *Art and Law*, (1) 2020, Leiden Boston: Brill 1–139.

Perraya Aaron and Margoni Thomas, "From music tracks to Google Maps: Who owns computer generated works?" 26 *Comp. L. and Sec. Rev.* 2010.

Peukert Alexander "A Doctrine of the Public Domain", in Josef Drexl and Anselm Kamperman (eds.) *The Innovation Society and Public Policy* 2019, 117–145.

Pierre Barbara, "Classification of Property and Conceptions of Ownership in Civil and Common Law" 28 *Revue générale de droit* 1997, 235–274.

Ramalho Ana, "*Will robots rule the (artistic) world? A proposed model for the legal status of creations by artificial intelligence systems*, 2017. https://papers.ssrn.com/sol3/papers.cfm?abstract_id=2987757.

Ricolfi Marco, "Towards an EU Co Code? A Conceptual Framework", Irina Stamatoudi, *New Developments in EU and International Copyright Law*, Kluwer: New York, 2016, Ch.18.

Ritchie Graeme, "Some Empirical Criteria for Attributing Creativity to A Computer Program", 17 *Minds and Machines* 2007, 67–99.

Russell Stuart P. and Norvig Peter, *Artificial Intelligence. A modern approach,* 4rd ed., London: Pearson 2020.

Samuelson Pamela "Allocating Ownership Rights in Computer Generated Works" 47 *U.Pitt.L.Rev.* 1985, 1185.

Sawyer Robert Keith, *Explaining Creativity: The Science of Human Innovation*, Oxford: OUP, 2012.

Searle John, *The Construction of Social Reality*, New York: Free Press, 1995.

Smith Sylvia, "Iamus: Is this the 21st century's answer to Mozart?" BBC News (Jan. 3, 2013), http://www.bbc.com/news/technology-20889644.

Solaiman Sheikh, "Legal personality of robots, corporations, idols and chimpanzees: a quest for legitimacy", 25 *Artif. Intell. Law* 2017, 155–179.

Solum Lawrence, "Legal Personhood for Artificial Intelligences", 70 *North Carolina L. Rev.* 1992, 1231–1287.

Thaler Stephen, "Neural Networks that Autonomously Create and Discover", http://imagination-engines.com/iei_pcai.php[https://perma.cc/52TZ-GPNB] (last visited 13.01.2020).

Thoma Martin, "Creativity in Machine Learning", *arXiv: 1601.03642v1* [*cs.CV*] (January 12, 2016).

Turing Alan, "Computer Machinery and Intelligence", *Mind* (October 1950), 433.

Ubertazzi Luigi Carlo "IP and the Draft Treaty on the EU", 38 IIC – Int. R. IP & Comp. L. 2007), 881.

Volland Holger, *Die kreative Macht der Maschinen*, Basel: Beltz Verlag, 2018.

Yanisky-Ravid Shlomit "Generating Rembrandt: Artificial Intelligence, Copyright, and Accountability in the 3d Era. The Human-Like Authors Are Already Here", 90 *Mich. St. L. Rev.* 2017, 659.

Zemer Lior, *The Idea of Authorship in Copyright*, London: Routledge, 2016.

Zemer Lior, "Rethinking Copyright Alternatives", 14 *International Journal of Law and Information Technology* 2006, 137–145.

Zibner Jan, "Artificial Intelligence: A Creative Player in the Game of Copyright" 10 *Eur. J. of L. & Tech.*, 1, 2019, 1–16.

www.ingramcontent.com/pod-product-compliance
Lightning Source LLC
Chambersburg PA
CBHW071357230926
51846CB00002B/581
* 9 7 8 9 0 0 4 4 4 2 6 6 5 *